FaithWords

LARGE PRINT

The
Power
-of-
Thank
You

Discover the Joy of Gratitude

JOYCE MEYER

LARGE ❤ PRINT

FaithWords
Hachette Book Group
1290 Avenue of the Americas, New York, NY 10104
faithwords.com
twitter.com/faithwords

First Edition: January 2022

FaithWords is a division of Hachette Book Group, Inc.

The FaithWords name and logo are trademarks of Hachette Book Group, Inc.

The publisher is not responsible for websites (or their content) that are not owned by the publisher.

The Hachette Speakers Bureau provides a wide range of authors for speaking events. To find out more, go to www.hachettespeakersbureau.com or call (866) 376-6591.

Library of Congress Cataloging-in-Publication Data
Names: Meyer, Joyce, 1943- author.
Title: The power of thank you : discover the joy of gratitude / Joyce Meyer.
Description: First edition. | New York : FaithWords, [2022] |
Identifiers: LCCN 2021033002 | ISBN 9781546016120 (hardcover) |
ISBN 9781546001065 (large type) | ISBN 9781546016137 (ebook)
Subjects: LCSH: Gratitude—Religious aspects—Christianity. | Joy—Religious aspects—Christianity.
Classification: LCC BV4647.G8 M494 2022 | DDC 179/.9—dc23
LC record available at https://lccn.loc.gov/2021033002

ISBNs: 978-1-5460-1612-0 (hardcover), 978-1-5460-0106-5 (large type), 978-1-5460-0227-7 (international trade), 978-1-5460-0260-4 (signed edition), 978-1-5460-0260-4 (Barnes & Noble.com edition), 978-1-5460-1613-7 (ebook)

Printed in the United States of America

LSC-C

Printing 1, 2021

CONTENTS

INTRODUCTION

I am excited about writing on the subject of thankfulness because I think having a grateful heart has more power than we can imagine. Being thankful is obviously important because God's Word is filled with instructions and reminders to give thanks and be thankful. The words *thanks* and *thanksgiving* appear in approximately one hundred verses in the Bible, and we are told to give thanks seventy-three times. I believe that anything the Holy Spirit repeats that often must be important to my life and yours.

We are to have thankful hearts and express our thankfulness to God and to the people in our lives who help us, encourage us, and do things for us. Psalm 100:4 states that we should "be thankful and say so" (AMPC). I like this scripture because it reminds me that people can't read my mind. They need me to communicate my gratitude in order to know that I appreciate them and am thankful for them.

As we read the Old Testament, we find that possibly the Israelites' biggest problem may have been that they initially gave thanks for God's goodness to them but quickly forgot Him and went back to complaining and disobedience. Over and over God forgave them when they repented, and then they repeated the same process of being thankful, forgetting God, and going back into bondage. When God did mighty works for the Israelites, Psalm 106:12–13 says, "They believed his promises and sang his praise. But they soon forgot what he had done and did not wait for his plan to unfold."

God brought thousands of people out of bondage in Egypt, and they headed toward the Promised Land. One reason only two men out of that large group—Joshua and Caleb— actually entered the Promised Land was that so many of the others complained instead of being thankful. Some of those born in the wilderness did enter into the Promised Land with Joshua and Caleb, but the rest were destroyed, partially due to a lack of gratitude, which led to disobedience to God. This shows the power of thank you.

The apostle Paul teaches us that God's will

for us is to be thankful at all times in everything (1 Thessalonians 5:18). I admit that this is a tall order, but God never asks us to do anything we cannot do with His help.

My goal in this book is to birth in you a fresh revelation of the power of being thankful and urge you to make a new and firm commitment to being more thankful than you have ever been. I truly believe that the words *thank you* contain power that will change your life. I have concentrated on being thankful for a long time, and I can testify that thankfulness releases joy in our lives, has a powerful effect on our prayers, and keeps us focused on the positive aspects of our lives.

Our gratitude belongs first to God, because without Him we would have nothing. God is good. Goodness is part of His character and essence, and He is good all the time. He desires our good and wants us to be good to others. Where goodness flows forth, thankfulness should also flow forth. When we stop seeing the good in our lives and start complaining, we cause many problems for ourselves. I like to say, "Why be grumpy when we can be grateful?"

I look forward to hearing about how this

book helps you become a more thankful person. I am thankful that you are reading it and
thankful that God has allowed me to write it. I
begin it leaning entirely on Him for the words
He wants to speak to you through it.

The
Power
-of-
Thank
You

CHAPTER 1

Thankfulness Is God's Will

Thank [God] in everything [no matter what the circumstances may be, be thankful and give thanks], for this is the will of God for you [who are] in Christ Jesus [the Revealer and Mediator of that will].

1 Thessalonians 5:18 AMPC

Because God does so much for us, we should be thankful in every circumstance, even if everything is not pleasant for us at the moment. No matter what kind of difficulty we may face, our blessings always outweigh our troubles. We create problems for ourselves when we forget our blessings or begin to take them for granted because we have had them for so long. When this happens, we begin to focus only on life's difficulties.

> No matter what kind of difficulty we may face, our blessings always outweigh our troubles.

God doesn't need us to thank Him, so I imagine His instructions to do so are repeated frequently because expressing our gratitude is good for us. It keeps us focused on our blessings instead of our problems, which adds joy and contentment to our lives. Studies have shown that thankful people tend to be healthier than those who complain frequently.

The story in Luke 17:11–19 (ESV) gives us

an idea of how few people take time to give thanks:

> On the way to Jerusalem he was passing along between Samaria and Galilee. And as he entered a village, he was met by ten lepers, who stood at a distance and lifted up their voices, saying, "Jesus, Master, have mercy on us." When he saw them he said to them, "Go and show yourselves to the priests." And as they went they were cleansed. Then one of them, when he saw that he was healed, turned back, praising God with a loud voice; and he fell on his face at Jesus' feet, giving him thanks. Now he was a Samaritan. Then Jesus answered, "Were not ten cleansed? Where are the nine? Was no one found to return and give praise to God except this foreigner?" And he said to him, "Rise and go your way; your faith has made you well."

As you can see, Jesus cleanses ten lepers of the horrible disease of leprosy, but only one returns to say thank you. I can't help but wonder what happened to the other nine lepers Jesus healed. The Bible doesn't tell us, but it is definitely food for thought.

Thankfulness Is a Sign of Spiritual Maturity

Giving thanks in all things at all times shows spiritual maturity, and it is something we grow into little by little. We are not born as thankful people, but we can cultivate a culture of gratitude in our lives. In the early stages of our relationship with God

> Giving thanks in all things at all times shows spiritual maturity.

through Christ, we may not be aware of all the amazing ways He helps and blesses us on a regular basis; we may be more inclined to notice what we don't like about our lives and want God to fix. But as we grow in our knowledge of God and in His blessings, we realize that the list of things we have to be thankful for is endless, even in the midst of our problems. As I often say, our worst day with Jesus is better than our best day ever was without Him. Take a few moments right now and think of all the things God provides, such as:

- peace
- answered prayer
- grace
- forgiveness of sin
- hope
- right relationship with Him through Christ
- provision
- mercy
- help
- wisdom
- strength
- and many other blessings

Even if all your problems vanished right now, if you had none of these blessings I have listed as gifts from God, I am sure you would rather keep your problem with the blessings of God than get rid of the problem and lose the blessings too.

As I have studied the apostle Paul's writings, I have learned that he never prayed for people's problems to go away. This is also a sign of spiritual maturity. He prayed they would bear whatever they had to endure with good attitudes.

In his epistles to the churches, he frequently reminded people to be thankful. In his letter to the Colossians alone, instructions to be thankful are plentiful:

> We always thank God, the Father of our Lord Jesus Christ, when we pray for you, because we have heard of your faith in Christ Jesus and of the love you have for all God's people.
>
> Colossians 1:3–4

> Giving joyful thanks to the Father, who has qualified you to share in the inheritance of his holy people in the kingdom of light. For he has rescued us from the dominion of darkness and brought us into the kingdom of the Son he loves, in whom we have redemption, the forgiveness of sins.
>
> Colossians 1:12–14

> So then, just as you received Christ Jesus as Lord, continue to live your lives in him, rooted and built up in him, strengthened in the faith as you were taught, and overflowing with thankfulness.
>
> Colossians 2:6–7

Let the peace of Christ rule in your hearts, since as members of one body you were called to peace. And be thankful. Let the message of Christ dwell among you richly as you teach and admonish one another with all wisdom through psalms, hymns, and songs from the Spirit, singing to God with gratitude in your hearts. And whatever you do, whether in word or deed, do it all in the name of the Lord Jesus, giving thanks to God the Father through him.

Colossians 3:15–17

Devote yourselves to prayer, being watchful and thankful.

Colossians 4:2

As you can see, in this one epistle, which consists of only four chapters, Paul encourages the giving of thanks several times. This tells me that we need frequent reminders to be thankful.

In Ephesians 5:20 Paul pens these simple yet powerful words: "Always giving thanks to God the Father for everything, in the name of our Lord Jesus Christ." He urges his readers to be thankful in most of his epistles, and I think reading his letters looking for instructions to be thankful would be enlightening and encouraging for you.

Some scholars and Bible teachers refer to Paul as "the apostle of thanksgiving." No wonder he was trusted to write two-thirds of the New Testament. Paul had experienced God's great grace and mercy at his conversion on the Damascus road, and we can tell from his writings that he never stopped being thankful for it (Acts 9:3–5). We should follow his example and never stop being thankful for all that God does in our lives and the blessings He gives to us.

A Story of Heartfelt Thanks

I recently read an article about a homeless man who was often hungry, cold, tired, and in poor health. He had no family and, apparently, no one to love him. The author of the article had previously read about this homeless person and wrote:

> It broke my heart that anyone who is homeless has to go through such circumstances. However, one might think the man

would give up hope, become bitter, angry, depressed and lonely because life appears to have dealt him a bad hand, right? Instead, the article went on to say how the man makes a point every day to go feed the birds with crumbs or food that he can find in the trash or if a Good-Samaritan offers him some food, he shares it. He was asked how he felt about being homeless and he replied, "I have the air in my lungs and I'm grateful for everything I have been blessed with but most important I am grateful for three things: that I'm alive, that I have the ability to love," *(and with tears starting to fill his eyes)* his third gratitude…"that I have my beloved birds."[1]

This story is very touching, and it makes me want to go help someone. Anyone who has such a good attitude while living under such circumstances should inspire each of us. Just think of the small issues we complain about in relation to the blessings for which this homeless man was thankful. His gratitude gave him the power to be happy in the midst of very difficult situations.

The Power of Thank You

Many people are taught as children to give thanks at mealtime. Although this is good, we should also be taught from an early age to give thanks in all things. The giving of thanks is powerful beyond what we may realize. It brings many benefits to our lives and to the lives of other people. Gratitude to God makes our relationship with Him better, and expressing appreciation and thanks to others certainly improves our relationships with them.

When we do something for someone and they don't even bother to acknowledge it with a thank you, we can feel that the gesture has fallen flat. I don't do things for people in order to get thanks from them, yet it still feels as though something is missing when they do not express appreciation for what I have done. I feel they are missing a blessing by "taking" or receiving something without acknowledging their gratitude. Perhaps they have never been taught regarding the importance of expressing gratitude. If not, it is never too late to learn.

I never want to fail to say thank you, but I am sure that I sometimes neglect to do so; therefore,

I am writing this book for myself as well as for you. As I mentioned earlier, Psalm 100:4 says that we are to "be thankful and say so" (AMPC). This is a simple, yet powerful instruction. It means to have a heart that appreciates everything it is given and a mouth that expresses thanksgiving to God and to people through words.

Nehemiah 8:10 says that the joy of the Lord is our strength. Expressing gratitude through phrases such as *thank you* or *I appreciate you* not only blesses those to whom we speak, but it also releases something powerful in us. It helps us realize how blessed we are, and keeping that in mind gives us joy. I think speaking words of gratitude in person is the best option when possible, but we may also choose to text, email, call, or write a note to people we want to thank. Doing so takes very little time and does us a great deal of good. It is not happy people who are thankful; it is thankful people who are happy.

> It is not happy people who are thankful; it is thankful people who are happy.

I have heard that one of the deepest needs in human beings is to be appreciated. Charles Schwab said, "The way to develop the best that

is in a person is by appreciation and encouragement." No one wants to feel taken advantage of
or to sense that what they do for others is mean-
ingless. But when people do not express gratitude, it is easy for our enemy, Satan, to whisper
in our ears, "You don't really matter. What you
did for them didn't make any difference." We
have the power to help others avoid such negative feelings by simply saying thank you when it
should be said. I suspect we could spare people
many of the enemy's lies by simply being more
encouraging and appreciative.

We have the ability to give people value with
our words. Isn't that amazing? Words are con-
tainers for power, and we can choose the type of
power we will put into them. This power can be
positive in its ability to build up and encourage
people or negative in its capacity to tear down
and discourage them.

Although we should listen more than we talk
(James 1:19), there are times we should speak,
and one of those times is to
say thank you. Silent gratitude
doesn't do much for anyone.
When was the last time you
said you were thankful for

> Silent gratitude doesn't do much for anyone.

something or someone? If it has been a while, maybe now would be a good time.

Expressing thankfulness can greatly improve your marriage. Just imagine how your life with your spouse might change if you began to appreciate them more than you find fault with them. Great things could happen. Gratitude can melt a hard heart and heal emotional wounds. I recall a time when I was unhappy with Dave and thinking about everything that I thought was wrong with him. I felt the Lord challenge me to write a list of everything I didn't like about him, along with everything I did like. When I had finished, I realized I liked much more about him than I didn't like, and it turned my whole attitude around.

Nobody is perfect—not even you and me.

Get Your Mind off of Yourself

Being thankful keeps our focus off ourselves and on what God and other people do for us. As I write this book, my daughter and son-in-law are with me. They are here for one purpose—to help me. They do everything so that I am free to write, and I am thankful. They just told me that they will pay for dinner tonight, so there is another blessing for which I can thank God and them. No wonder the Bible encourages us to count our blessings and to "praise the

> *Being thankful keeps our focus off ourselves and on what God and other people do for us.*

Lord...and forget not all his benefits" (Psalm 103:2).

If we actually pay attention to all that God does for us and count our blessings, it will definitely help us keep our mind off ourselves. Being self-centered and happy at the same time is impossible. I know, because I tried it for years. Thank God, He showed me that the less I think about myself, the happier I am and the more He will do for me. I don't ignore my legitimate needs, but I do make an effort not to think I am the only person in the universe who matters.

Paul writes in Philippians 2:3: "Do nothing out of selfish ambition or vain conceit. Rather, in humility value others above yourselves." And in 1 Corinthians 10:24, he says: "No one should seek their own good, but the good of others." These verses don't mean that we should never do anything good for ourselves, but they do mean that our personal benefit should not be our only goal. The more we bless others, the more blessed we will be.

If we think often of what we have, we won't end up wanting more and more all the time, which leads to unhappiness. Greed steals our life, according to Proverbs 1:10–19. It prevents us from seeing our current blessings and keeps us focused only on what we want but do not have.

Let me encourage you to begin to cultivate a culture of thanksgiving in your life by going through your day being thankful for every blessing you have, especially the tiny ones that many people tend to take for granted. This will add power to your life and bring you closer to God. Thanksgiving is a type of praise, and the Bible says that we enter God's gates with thanksgiving and come into His courts with praise (Psalm 100:4).

CHAPTER 2

Gratitude and Contentment

He who is not contented with what he has, would not be contented with what he would like to have.

Socrates

Paul was an extremely thankful man. He was also satisfied with his life and said that he had learned to be content whether he was abased or abounding, meaning whether he had little or much (Philippians 4:11). Just imagine being content regardless of your circumstances! I think gratitude and contentment go hand in hand; therefore, grumbling and discontentment must also go hand in hand.

I sometimes find myself discontented for no reason at all. God has blessed me immeasurably. I have a wonderful family and the best job in the world, so why would I be dissatisfied? Simply because I sometimes fail to be thankful for things I should be thankful for but take for granted instead.

For example, I received two gifts this morning as soon as I woke up: my eyes. This morning I thanked God that I could see, hear, think, talk, and walk. Just imagine how we would complain and how challenging our lives would be if we couldn't do any of these, and yet we rarely thank God for the ability to do them.

Gratitude Is Part of Our New Nature

An attitude of discontentment is part of our old nature rather than part of the new nature God gives us when we are born again (2 Corinthians 5:17). Even though we consider that old nature to have been crucified with Christ (Galatians 2:20), it often comes back for a visit, and we must remind it that it is not welcome. When we receive Jesus as our Lord and Savior, we are said to be dead to sin, but I have realized that sin is not necessarily dead to us.

> The death he died, he died to sin once for all; but the life he lives, he lives to God. In the same way, count yourselves dead to sin but alive to God in Christ Jesus. Therefore do not let sin reign in your mortal body so that you obey its evil desires.
>
> Romans 6:10–12

To count ourselves dead to sin does not mean we won't be tempted. It means that when sin does tempt us, we should not let it reign and obey its evil desires. The devil delights in trying to make us discontent. He knows that if he succeeds, he will keep us from being thankful. Being thankful gives us power, and the devil wants to keep us weak. He attempts to blind us to what we have to be thankful for, and he tempts us to always want something else that we think will make us happy.

To be content means to be satisfied to the point where you are not upset or disturbed. Let me ask you: Can you be satisfied with what God has given you at this time in your life? If you can, then eventually you will be blessed with more.

> Can you be satisfied with what God has given you at this time in your life?

I believe that being discontent is disrespectful to the Lord, because He is so good to us. Jesus died for us and took all the punishment we deserved as sinners, and He rose from the dead so we might live a resurrection life and spend eternity with Him. This truth alone should be enough to keep us thankful all of our lives, even if we never have anything else.

In fact, God's Word tells us to be content if we simply have food and clothing:

> But godliness with contentment is great gain, for we brought nothing into the world, and we cannot take anything out of the world.

> But if we have food and clothing, with these
> we will be content.
>
> 1 Timothy 6:6–8 ESV

Because of the abundance to which we have become accustomed, I seriously doubt that anyone in our culture could be content if food and clothing were all they had. Food and clothes are not all that God wants for us, but He does want us to trust Him and believe that He will always give us what we need at the right time. He gives us more as we are able to handle it and still keep Him first in our lives. We are often guilty of asking God to give us things that we are not spiritually mature enough to handle properly. Ask God for what you want and need, and then trust His timing to be perfect in your life.

> Beloved, I pray that you may prosper in every
> way and [that your body] may keep well,
> even as [I know] your soul keeps well and
> prospers.
>
> 3 John 2 AMPC

A prosperous soul is a mature one. God wants us to be abundantly blessed, but He won't give us material blessings that are beyond our spiritual maturity to manage well. Don't merely pray for possessions, but first pray to be all that God wants you to be and to represent Him well in all you do. Pray to walk in the fruit of the Spirit, and let love be the number one goal in your life. When we seek first God's kingdom and His way of being and doing, He promises to add everything else to us (Matthew 6:33).

Jesus died so we might have life and have it in abundance (John 10:10), and God refers to Himself as El Shaddai, which means "the God of more than enough" (Exodus 6:3 AMPC). He is able to do "superabundantly, far over and above all that we [dare] ask or think" (Ephesians 3:20 AMPC). If we delight ourselves in Him, He will give us the desires of our heart (Psalm 37:4).

Seek God's Presence, Not His Presents

We should desire God for Himself, not merely for what He can do for us. As a baby Christian, I constantly asked God to give me worldly goods and do things for me or bless me in certain ways. I wanted more money. I wanted my ministry to be large and successful, and at the time I was teaching a small home Bible study group. I wanted Dave to change and be more like I was. I wanted my children to be little angels who always pleased me in all their ways. I wanted and wanted and wanted—and was frustrated and discontent most of the time.

I loved the Lord, but not fully as He desired for me to love Him.

> Jesus replied: " 'Love the Lord your God with all your heart and with all your soul and with all your mind.' This is the first and greatest commandment. And the second is like it: 'Love your neighbor as yourself.' "
> Matthew 22:37–39

As we continue seeking God, we grow spiritually and learn what is truly important. In my life, a time came when God revealed to me that I was unhappy because I was seeking the wrong things. I believe I was reading *The Practice of the Presence of God* by Brother Lawrence when my eyes were opened to the discontentment I felt. I realized that even though I spent time in prayer regularly, most of my prayers were selfish and materialistic.

This was a turning point in my walk with God, and my joy increased greatly when I finally focused on praying for the things God wanted me to pray for.

> *As we continue seeking God, we grow spiritually and learn what is truly important.*

In Psalm 27, David desired "one thing." All he sought was to dwell in God's presence and see His beauty "all the days" of his life (Psalm 27:4). One thing! Truly, there is only one thing that can keep us content, which is to keep God first in all we do, all the time. If and when we put Him first, all the other aspects of our lives work themselves out. They may not work out exactly as we hope, but eventually we realize that God's ways are always better than ours.

I recall God challenging me not to ask Him for anything other than more of Himself until He released me to do so. Each time I started to ask for something, the words stuck in my throat and I would say, "Never mind, Lord, I just need more of You." This lasted for about six months. By then, my heart had been changed drastically, and I might add that God has blessed me with more of the items I had previously asked for because I sought His presence, not His presents.

The word *presence* means "face" and represents a close, personal relationship with God. His presence should be our number one desire. God's presence is everywhere because He is omnipresent; He is never more than one thought away from us. We can simply think of God and immediately bring Him into our conscious awareness. God's presence not only fills the earth (Isaiah 11:9), but it also fills every believer (John 14:16–17). We may at times *feel* God's presence, but more often than not we accept by faith the truth that He is always present.

Of course, we would prefer some kind of experience with God that assures us that He is with us. We would like a burning bush, or an instant healing from disease, or an ocean that parts so we can walk through it on dry ground. We love goose bumps and feelings of electricity running through our bodies. I've heard people speak of having all kinds of physical experiences of God's presence, including Jesus sitting with them for hours, showing them future events. As exciting as this must be, I tend to think that if we had remarkable manifestations of God's presence all the time, we would begin to require them in order to believe, and that is not God's will.

Hebrews 11:6 emphasizes our need for faith,

saying: "Without faith it is impossible to please God, because anyone who comes to him must believe that he exists and that he rewards those who earnestly seek him." I don't put too much emphasis on such physical experiences, because although they can be genuine, they can also be merely emotional. Therefore, we need to use caution and not put too much confidence in them. The devil can easily deceive people through their emotions.

I have heard God's voice a few times in forty-seven years, and much time has passed between each of those instances. He does speak to me all the time, but He speaks in my heart, in a still, small voice that whispers so softly that I must receive it by faith. He also speaks to me through His Word and through what I call a "knowing." I simply have a deep knowing that He either wants me to do or not to do something. I believe He also leads all of us by peace or the absence of it, and He leads us through wisdom.

I've enjoyed some very exciting times with God, but most of my life—probably like yours— is quite ordinary. Of course, with God in it, it is extraordinary, but my point is that we normally don't live from one high to another because of visions and special experiences. I've learned to trust that God will give me what I need when I need it. Should I truly need a burning bush, I am convinced He would provide one. I do see the evidence of God in my life regularly through answered prayer and provision, strength beyond what I possess, and creativity I know is not natural for me. I also see His favor, and I greatly appreciate it.

James 4:2 says that we have not because we ask not, so it is certainly good to ask God for anything we want or need, but more frequently we should ask for more of Him. Praise should outweigh petition, and our prayers should be heavily laden with thanksgiving.

Fully Satisfied

The *American Heritage Dictionary* defines *content* as "desiring no more than what one has; satisfied." We might also use the words *fulfilled, adequate,* or *sufficient* to convey the idea of contentment. Being content does not mean that we never want anything to change or improve for us. We can want change in the future while also being content with the present if we believe God's timing in our lives is perfect.

For the vision is yet for an appointed time
and it hastens to the end [fulfillment]; it
will not deceive or disappoint. Though it
tarry, wait [earnestly] for it, because it will
surely come; it will not be behindhand on
its appointed day.

Habakkuk 2:3 AMPC

Ecclesiastes 3 teaches us that there is a perfect time for everything and that everything is
beautiful in its time (Ecclesiastes 3:1, 11). Being
out of God's timing is equivalent to being out
of His will. Think of Abraham and Sarah, who
developed and followed their own plan to have
the child God had promised them, and consider
how many problems this caused. Genesis 16 tells
us that Sarah had the idea that Abraham could
take her handmaid Hagar as a secondary wife
and Sarah could have a child through her (v. 2).
However, when Hagar became pregnant, she
despised Sarah (v. 4), and much trouble started.
Sarah mistreated Hagar, who ran away into the
wilderness (v. 6). The angel of the Lord found
Hagar and told her to go back to her mistress
(vv. 7–9), saying:

You are now pregnant and you will give birth to a son. You shall name him Ishmael, for the Lord has heard of your misery. He will be a wild donkey of a man; his hand will be against everyone and everyone's hand against him, and he will live in hostility toward all his brothers.

Genesis 16:11–12

Ishmael was a man of war, and conflict accompanied him throughout his lifetime.

God's promised child was named Isaac, and his name meant "laughter." When we try to make something happen for ourselves ahead of God's timing, we end up with Ishmael—war and torment. But when we wait on God, we have laughter and joy.

> Be content with what you have right now, knowing that God has a perfect timing for the things you do not have yet.

Be content with what you have right now, knowing that God has a perfect timing for the things you do not have yet.

This scripture has meant a lot to me and I read it often, especially if I begin to feel discontented:

As for me, I will continue beholding Your face in righteousness (rightness, justice, and right standing with You); I shall be fully satisfied, when I awake [to find myself] beholding Your form [and having sweet communion with You].

Psalm 17:15 AMPC

When I teach on the subject of contentment, people often ask, "How can I be content when my circumstances are so terrible?" One way is to be thankful for what you do have and focus on that. Everyone can find something positive for which to be grateful, even under difficult circumstances. We can't find satisfaction if we look for it in our circumstances, because they are rarely all we would want them to be, but the scripture above does tell us how to find it: by living in God's presence.

Gratitude: The Antidote for Discontentment

I truly believe that the more grateful we are, the less discontentment we will experience.

I once heard a story that makes a good point about this. A man and his sister had not been close for a while because he had moved out of the country and they rarely saw one another. The sister took care of their mother, and although he was grateful that she did, he had never expressed it to her. He decided to send her a text telling her how much he appreciated all she did, and he noticed that as soon as he hit the Send button, he felt a burst of joy. His intention was to encourage his sister and add to her joy, and I'm sure he did, but the lesson is that by expressing gratitude he received joy himself.

I think we can use gratitude in our hearts as we would use a medicine for pain or for an illness in our bodies. Discontentment is an illness of the soul, and when we have an attack of it, large doses of gratitude will heal it. God promises to heal our wounded souls, but this often requires our taking some God-inspired action. I think purposeful gratitude and giving of thanks is the antidote we need for discontentment.

> Discontentment is an illness of the soul, and when we have an attack of it, large doses of gratitude will heal it.

CHAPTER 3

Be Thankful that Roses Have Thorns

The optimist sees the rose and not its thorns; the pessimist stares at the thorns, oblivious to the rose.

Kahlil Gibran

The rose is certainly one of the most beautiful and desired flowers God has created, yet every rose grows with thorns. Life is much the same, I think, and each of us must decide if we can be thankful for the rose while dealing with the thorns.

The apostle James teaches that we should be exceedingly joyful in our trials, knowing that they will work good in us (James 1:2–4). The good that comes from them is perseverance, or endurance. I would define *endurance* as the ability to remain emotionally stable and spiritually mature and continuing to do right, even when you are hurt-

> The less we become upset about difficulty, the easier it is to deal with.

ing. No one enjoys difficulty, but the less upset we become about it, the easier it is to deal with.

I have come to believe that we would have no appreciation or gratitude for life's good times if we never experienced difficulties. Many of us are extremely grateful for all that God has done for us in Christ because we did have difficult and painful lives. God has given us "beauty for ashes," as He promised (Isaiah 61:3 NKJV), meaning that He has taken all the ugliness we have experienced in life and created something beautiful from it.

God has delivered us and taken what Satan meant for harm and worked it for our good. This idea comes from the Old Testament story of Joseph. You can read this entire story in Genesis 37–50, but I will summarize the key points here.

Joseph's brothers were so jealous of him that they sold him into slavery in Egypt, where he suffered for many years (Genesis 37:1–11, 26–28; 39:11–20). Ultimately, God moved on Joseph's behalf and he ended up second-in-command to Pharaoh (Genesis 41:41). God provided him with the wisdom and strategy to store vast supplies of grain in Egypt, and when famine struck Egypt and the surrounding nations, people came to him for grain (Genesis 41:46–49, 57). His brothers traveled to Egypt looking for food, but they did not recognize him because so many years had passed since they had seen him. When he did reveal himself to them, they were "terrified at his presence" (Genesis 45:3). Although he immediately expressed kindness toward them, they soon became afraid he would seek revenge on them (Genesis 50:15). He did not. He saw God's hand in the situation and said that what they meant to harm him, God intended for good (Genesis 50:19–20).

There is nothing bad that can happen to you that God cannot turn into something good, just as He did for Joseph. Not only did the situation ultimately turn out well for Joseph himself, but it also enabled him to save many people's lives, including his own family's lives, during a severe famine (Genesis 50:20). You may not yet be able to see how your trial or problem could become a blessing, but have faith and trust God to create beauty out of the suffering. Develop and maintain a thankful heart in the midst of it, and you will be amazed by the way God can use it for good.

Thorns to Roses

In Luke's gospel, we find a beautiful account of a sinful woman who came to Jesus while He was a guest at the house of a Pharisee named Simon (Luke 7:36–50). She came with an alabaster jar of perfume, which, according to historians, was worth about one year's wages. Verse 38 says,

"As she stood behind him at his feet weeping, she began to wet his feet with her tears. Then she wiped them with her hair, kissed them and poured perfume on them." In case you wonder how she could stand behind Him and be at His feet, she could do so because He was there for a meal and people in His culture stretched out on couches as they ate, probably propped up on one elbow.

The Pharisees were shocked and indignant that Jesus would allow a sinful woman like this to touch Him. In addition, she had let down her hair to wipe His feet, and a woman in those times did not ever let down her hair in public because it was considered indecent. She broke all the rules of her time in order to get to Jesus and show her love for Him. I think we too could get a bit radical if we love Jesus enough.

Jesus chastised the Pharisees for their judgmental attitude, reminding them that they didn't even offer Him water to wash His feet when He entered the house, but that she had washed them with her tears. He said, "You did not give me a kiss, but this woman, from the time I entered, has not stopped kissing my feet. You did not put oil on my head, but she has poured perfume on my feet" (Luke 7:45–46). Then He said, "Therefore, I tell you, her many sins have been forgiven—as her great love has shown. But whoever has been forgiven little loves little" (Luke 7:47).

This story contains several wonderful messages, one of which is that those who have received the most help will love the most. This woman was extremely thankful for what Jesus had done for her because her sin had been great. I am extremely thankful for what Jesus has done for me because not only was my sin great, but I also experienced a great deal of abuse and unjust treatment in my life.

God has brought me through a lot, and as Daniel 3:27 says of Shadrach, Meshach, and Abednego, who were delivered from the fiery furnace, I don't even smell like smoke! In other words, to look at my life now, no one would ever imagine the condition I was in when I turned my life over to Jesus. I had thorns for many years, but I have found the roses, and I can say without hesitation that everything I have been through was worth it because of the gratitude I now have for God's goodness in my life.

Author and coach Marc Chernoff had a conversation with his wise seventy-one-year-old father about life and growing through adversity, and said this about it:

> One of the last things he said before we got off the phone resonated so much with me that I wrote it down. "It's been my experience that most people aren't truly happy until they've had many reasons to be sad. I believe this is because it takes all of those bad days and hardships to teach us how to truly appreciate what we have. It builds our resilience."[2]

You Already Have the Victory

The psalmist David writes, "Even though I walk through the darkest valley, I will fear no evil, for you are with me" (Psalm 23:4).

Romans 8:37 says that we are "more than conquerors," and I think this means that we know we have victory over our difficulty before the trial ever begins. This kind of strong faith allows us to live without the fear of evil:

> Who shall separate us from the love of Christ? Shall trouble or hardship or persecution or

famine or nakedness or danger or sword?
As it is written: "For your sake we face
death all day long; we are considered as sheep
to be slaughtered." No, in all these things
we are more than conquerors through him
who loved us.

Romans 8:35–37

I love this passage because it fills me with
hope while I am going through difficulties in
my life. We may appear to others as sheep being
led to the slaughter, but by faith we know that
we have victory. This knowledge allows us to be
thankful all the way through a trial to triumph.
While we are afflicted with thorns, we can enjoy
the roses!

Two other powerful scriptures that encourage
me are:

But thanks be to God! He gives us the
victory through our Lord Jesus Christ.

1 Corinthians 15:57

But thanks be to God, Who in Christ
always leads us in triumph [as trophies of
Christ's victory] and through us spreads

and makes evident the fragrance of the knowledge of God everywhere.

2 Corinthians 2:14 AMPC

> *When we remain faithful and thankful during our trials, people know that we belong to Jesus because we are displaying His character.*

When we remain faithful and thankful during our trials, people notice and know that we belong to Jesus because we are displaying His character. The world needs to hear about Jesus, but even more, it needs to see Him. The only way the world will see Him is through us.

How to Be Thankful through Difficult Times

I have walked with God for many years. I have a lot of experience with Him, and I know for certain that He always works all things out for good to those who love Him and want His will in their lives (Romans 8:28). Believing this allows us to remain thankful all the way through any unpleasant situation we face.

Job, whose story is in the Old Testament,

experienced terrible difficulties, yet he could still say:

> I know that my redeemer lives, and that in the end he will stand on the earth. And after my skin has been destroyed, yet in my flesh I will see God; I myself will see him with my own eyes—I, and not another. How my heart yearns within me!
>
> Job 19:25–27

What an amazing statement of faith. Job not only had lost everything, including his family and possessions, but he had also lost his health and was suffering with a skin disease that tormented him. An entire book of the Bible is devoted to Job, so powerful was his determination to choose thankfulness over despair.

God had said that Job was the most righteous person of his day (Job 1:8), but the problem was that Job knew it and was proud of it. This caused him to feel self-righteous rather than thanking God for who He is and for what He had done for him. God permitted trials in Job's life so that in the end he might be a better person—humble and free from self-righteousness.

We also learn from Job's story that bad things do happen to good people, and trying to understand why can be fruitless. God never really answered Job's complaints about what happened to him. He simply reminded him of who he was dealing with and asked Job several questions that basically told him he had no right to question Him (Job 38–42). When Job's ordeal was finished, God also gave him twice as much as he had lost (Job 42:10).

God wants us to trust Him, to know that anything we go through will work some good in our life, and to believe that when the trials are over, the smell of the roses of God's goodness will prevent us from focusing on the thorns of life.

A Test of Faith

Some of life's trials and tribulations are simply tests. They test our faith and spiritual maturity. When we are tested, we either grow stronger or recognize our weaknesses, enabling us to repent and allow God to work in those areas of our lives.

We are promised that if we withstand the tests we face, we will be rewarded.

Blessed is the one who perseveres under trial because, having stood the test, that person will receive the crown of life that the Lord has promised to those who love him.

James 1:12

In God's school, we never fail a test; we simply get to keep taking the same tests over and over until we pass. I always encourage myself and others to stand firm and pass the tests we face so we will not have to take them again.

> In God's school, we never fail a test; we simply get to keep taking the same tests over and over until we pass.

These trials are only to test your faith, to see whether or not it is strong and pure. It is being tested as fire tests gold and purifies it—and your faith is far more precious to God than mere gold; so if your faith remains strong after being tried in the test tube of fiery trials, it will bring you much praise and glory and honor on the day of his return.

1 Peter 1:7 TLB

Just as fire brings the impurities in gold to the surface, so our fiery trials bring our weaknesses into the open. Sometimes we imagine ourselves to be stronger and better than we are, just as Job did, so we can thank God for anything that tests our faith, trusting that it is for our benefit, not our destruction.

Today is a cloudy day where I am, and the previous few days have also been overcast. So I know I will appreciate the sun more when it does come out than I would have had I been through a week of bright, sunny days. Human nature seems to cause us to appreciate the good times more after we have experienced the challenging ones.

As I write this book, winter is right around the corner. My flowers have died, the leaves are mostly gone from the trees, the grass is no longer green, and lots of days are cloudy. But I know spring will come and summer will follow, and then fall, and finally winter again. My daughter and I have already talked about what kind of flowers we want to plant in the spring, and we are planning what we want to put in place of three diseased trees that had to be cut down.

Just as natural seasons change, so do the

seasons of our lives, and we can learn to appreciate and give thanks for all of them. In the difficult seasons, we can plan for the good times to come, because they certainly will.

Life Happens

Life happens to all of us, and not all of it is pretty. We face unexpected difficulties, but we also experience unexpected blessings. In life, there are flat tires, cars that won't start, co-workers we really don't like, neighbors who are annoying, and children and teenagers who simply don't seem to appreciate our wise advice. There are deaths we don't expect, jobs lost, bad reports from the doctor, and many other circumstances beyond our control. None of these challenges mean that we have done something wrong or even that God is trying to teach us a lesson. Nevertheless, we can determine to derive some good out of everything that comes our way. Good is released as we thank God in the midst of our difficulties, because even though life is sometimes unfair and

> We can determine to derive some good out of everything that comes our way.

very much a mystery, God is still good and we have much for which to be thankful.

While I was writing this book on being thankful, my refrigerator developed a problem. It took one week to get a repairman, and he replaced a part that caused another part to malfunction, so then we had to wait on that part. At the same time, I had a fever blister on my tongue and strained my back doing exercises.

In case you're still tempted to think that I just don't know what you are going through, let me share a little history from my life.

I was sexually abused by my father for approximately fifteen years. My mother was aware of the situation, but because she was afraid of him, she did nothing. I left home at age eighteen, as soon as I graduated high school. Soon afterward, I married the first boy who showed any interest in me. As it turned out, he had many issues and was dishonest and unfaithful. After five years of marriage, one miscarriage, and giving birth to a baby boy, I divorced that man.

I was close to being homeless except for the kindness of some people who heard about my situation. Thankfully, I did meet and quickly marry Dave, to whom I have been married since 1967. I was one huge thorn when we married, but thankfully Dave only saw roses. He loved God and he loved me unconditionally. This was the beginning of the healing of my wounded soul and broken life.

I've had breast cancer, two hip replacements, a minor back surgery, a hysterectomy, and a very difficult experience with menopause. I've experienced rejection, abandonment, abuse, betrayal, and lots of other unpleasant experiences. But I'm still here, and I love Jesus more than ever. I've had the great privilege of teaching God's Word for almost fifty years, and that alone has been worth anything I had to go through to get to where I am now.

This is my story in a nutshell, and I know you have your story, too. But our stories are still being written, so even if you don't like the first few chapters of yours, remember that your life isn't over yet. The ending is always the best part, and it will end well. You can begin thanking God now for all the good things that will show up in your future, because God's good plans have already been decreed for you in His Word:

"For I know the plans I have for you," declares the Lord, "plans to prosper you and not to harm you, plans to give you hope and a future."

Jeremiah 29:11

CHAPTER 4

Be Thankful and Say So

Feeling gratitude and not expressing it is like wrapping a present and not giving it.
William Arthur Ward

The mouth is the world's smallest large problem, meaning that while it's physically small, it does immense damage. But it doesn't have to. We can use our words for good or evil, so let's choose to use them for good. The way we choose to use our words can actually make us happier people. God gave us the same information long before scientists decided to agree.

> For let him who wants to enjoy life and see good days [good—whether apparent or not] keep his tongue free from evil and his lips from guile (treachery, deceit).
>
> 1 Peter 3:10 AMPC

Do you want to enjoy your life? If so, then it's necessary to keep your tongue free from evil, negative, and deceitful speech. James 3:8 says, "No human being can tame the tongue." No one can control your mouth for you. At the same time, no one can do it alone; we need *a lot* of help from God. In addition to needing His help to control our tongues, we also need a strong desire to please Him with our words. In addition, we need to understand the importance of words.

The psalmist David prayed about his words, and I pray his prayers for myself often. He asked God, "Set a guard over my mouth, Lord; keep watch over the door of my lips" (Psalm 141:3). He also prayed that his words and thoughts would be acceptable to God: "May these words of my mouth and this meditation of my heart be pleasing in your sight" (Psalm 19:14).

I borrow these prayers from David because I recognize that the power of my words not only affects others, but also affects me. Not only do others hear the words I speak, but I have to listen to everything I say. I believe that our words affect us more than we realize. If you know someone who seems to struggle or have trouble consistently, listen to what they normally say, and you will often find the cause of many of their problems.

I believe strongly in the power of words. The Bible tells us that the power of life and death is in our words.

> From the fruit of their mouth a person's stomach is filled; with the harvest of their lips they are satisfied. The tongue has the

power of life and death, and those who love
it will eat its fruit.

Proverbs 18:20–21

Proverbs, the Bible's book of wisdom, includes
numerous verses about the proper and improper
use of our words. As a matter of fact, it is a subject covered throughout the Bible. If you would
like to learn more about this, you can find exten-
sive teaching in my book *In Search of Wisdom*,
which takes you on a journey through the entire
book of Proverbs, or in the *Battlefield of the Mind
Bible*, which highlights many verses related to
thoughts and words.

Speak Your Gratitude

Forming the habit of speaking words of gratitude can greatly increase our happiness. People
may consider themselves to
be thankful, but if they
never "say so" (Psalm 100:4
AMPC), it doesn't do them
or anyone else much good.
Our thoughts become our
words, so if we are truly

> *Forming the habit
> of speaking words
> of gratitude can
> greatly increase
> our happiness.*

thankful, I don't see how we can keep quiet about it.

I like and agree with this advice and observation from Pastor Tim Dilena: "Go big with your thank yous. Author Gladys Bronwyn Stern said, 'Silent gratitude isn't much use to anyone.' True gratitude is vocal and focused."[3]

Psalm 136 includes twenty-six verses and begins with "Give thanks to the Lord, for he is good. His love endures forever." Each verse ends with "His love endures forever." We can speak to God aloud when we are alone, thanking Him for His never-ending love and for many other blessings.

Filling your day with the power of thank you improves your life immeasurably. It keeps you focused on the positive aspects of your life instead of the negative ones, and if you are thankful for what you have, God is more inclined to give you what you are asking for. One time I was asking God for something, and as He spoke to my heart, a thought came to me: *Why should I give you more if you are complaining about what you already have?*

For example, if you're complaining about your sore muscles after you work out, consider thanking God that you have the ability and energy to exercise. If you're complaining about unruly children, consider thanking God for the fact that you have a family. If you're complaining about the cost of a car repair, consider being thankful for a vehicle that could be fixed and become reliable again.

We usually think that having more will make us happy, but if we are not thankful for what we have, then having more won't change our attitude.

As you speak of your gratitude, remember to thank God often for His love, because it is the greatest gift we have. He loves us so much that He gave us His Son, Jesus, the greatest gift He could give. Jesus said, "As the Father has loved me, so have I loved you. Now remain in my love. If you keep my commands, you will remain in my love, just as I have kept my Father's commands and remain in his love. I have told you this so that my joy may be in you and that your joy may be complete" (John 15:-9–11). Recognizing, living, and remaining in God's love increases our joy. Jesus even says that it completes it. There is truly no way to be completely joyful unless we believe that God loves us unconditionally. And He does!

Declare God's Word

I love declaring God's Word aloud, and I believe there is great power in doing so. I believe that words have a creative force in them. God created the entire world in six days with nothing other than words, proving that they have creative power.

I don't believe, nor have I ever believed, that we can get anything we want simply by speaking it. But I do believe that if we cooperate with God by declaring His Word, it helps to bring His will to pass in our lives. The King James Version of the Bible says that angels hearken to the word of God (Psalm 103:20); this means they listen to the Word attentively and obey it. Therefore, when we speak His Word out of our mouths, angels can spring into action based on the words we speak. What angels don't do is hearken to complaints, grumbling, faultfinding, or any other negative or evil kind of speech.

Paul teaches in Romans 4:17 that God calls things that do not yet exist as though they do. He speaks the end from the beginning, because He is the end and the beginning, the Creator of all things. He called Abraham the father of many nations before he even had a child

(Genesis 17:4–5; Romans 4:16–18). God speaks in accordance with His planned outcome, and we should do the same. Don't keep talking about what you have that you don't like. Instead, talk about what you want and believe God is planning to do for you according to the promises in His Word.

Verbalize your gratitude frequently for little things and big things. Let words of thanksgiving weave their way through your day from the time you arise until you go to sleep. Let them be first on your lips when you awake and last before falling asleep. Remember, *thank you* is filled with power.

> *God speaks in accordance with His planned outcome, and we should do the same.*

Talking about Your Future

Let me ask you an important question: How do you talk about your future? God says that He has a good future planned for us, so no matter how difficult circumstances have been or currently are, we should declare that our future will be good. Believe that every word you speak has power in it. This will urge you to speak wisely rather than foolishly.

Here are a few scriptures to consider:

> The wise store up knowledge, but the mouth of a fool invites ruin.
>
> Proverbs 10:14

> The one who guards his mouth [thinking before he speaks] protects his life; the one who opens his lips wide [and chatters without thinking] comes to ruin.
>
> Proverbs 13:3 AMP

> A [self-confident] fool's lips bring contention, and his mouth invites a beating. A [self-confident] fool's mouth is his ruin, and his lips are a snare to himself.
>
> Proverbs 18:6–7 AMPC

> He who guards his mouth and his tongue keeps himself from troubles.
>
> Proverbs 21:23 AMPC

If you believe you might get what you say, if it's according to God's Word, you will take time to think before speaking. Say words that will help you and increase your joy. You only have one life to live, and God wants you to live wisely, be happy, and enjoy each day.

If you believe you might get what you say, if it's according to God's Word, you will take time to think before speaking.

Unwise Things People Say

I have made unwise comments at times, and I have heard others also say some things that are not wise. These would be classified as words of the foolish person and include remarks such as "I am sick and tired of this," "This is about to kill me," "My job drives me crazy," "I hate the way I look," or "Nothing will ever change in my stinking life."

Words such as these are filled with death, not life. They bring unhappiness, not happiness. It would be life-bringing to say instead, "I'm thankful I have a job," "I can do whatever I need to do through Christ who gives me strength" (see Philippians 4:13), or "God created me, and I believe everything He makes is good. That includes me!"

I hope you can begin to see what I am talking about. If you have been speaking negative words about your life and future, make a change and start right away to say what God says. Believe me, as you do this, you will see your joy and blessings increase.

Gratitude and Health

In reading about gratitude, I learned that grateful people may experience better sleep, have healthier hearts, and suffer from fewer aches and pains. They are happier and have better relationships. People are said to even exercise more if they are thankful. Perhaps doctors need to give out prescriptions for more gratitude instead of more medicine. It seems that everything improves for those who are thankful.

Consider this interesting scientific study:

In one study on gratitude, conducted by Robert A. Emmons, Ph.D., at the University of California Davis and his colleague Mike McCullough at the University of Miami, randomly assigned participants were given one of three tasks. Each week, participants kept a short journal. One group briefly described five things they were grateful for that had occurred in the past week, another five recorded daily hassles from the previous week that displeased them, and the neutral group was asked to list five events or circumstances that affected them, but they were not told whether to focus on the positive or on the negative. Ten weeks later, participants in the gratitude group felt better about their lives as a whole and were a full 25 percent happier than the hassled group. They reported fewer health complaints and exercised an average of 1.5 hours more.[4]

I highly recommend keeping a gratitude journal. Each day, write something for which you are thankful. When God blesses you in special ways, write them down, so you don't forget them. Anytime you start to feel discouraged or depressed, read your gratitude journal as soon as possible. Negative feelings are usually the result of focusing on negative situations or thoughts. But when we remember how much we have to be grateful for, we can stop negativity before it becomes a real problem.

People can actually become depressed due to thinking negatively. In all probability, anyone receiving psychological counseling for unhappiness or depression has been told to focus more on what they are thankful for. This alone may not solve their problems, but it should definitely be part of their overall program for healing. Being more thankful can have a positive effect on mental health, just as it does on physical health.

Gratitude also helps us relax. After all, isn't focusing on our problems what makes us tense and increases our stress? If you tend to be negative, becoming a thankful person who focuses on the positives in life will probably take some time and effort, but you can do it with God's help. All things are possible with God (Matthew 19:26).

If we could express what we want out of life in just a word, I think most of us would say that we want to be happy. Many roads lead to happiness, and being grateful is only one of them, but it is an important one. If you are an unhappy person, being thankful is probably a good place to begin your journey toward happiness.

G. K. Chesterton in *A Short History of England* wrote, "I would maintain that thanks are the highest form of thought; and that gratitude is happiness doubled by wonder." The *Oxford English Dictionary* defines the word *wonder* as "a feeling of surprise mingled with admiration, caused by something beautiful, unexpected, unfamiliar, or inexplicable." How many truly wonderful things would we recognize in our lives if we would only take the time to look for them? I think we would all be surprised by our blessings if we would count them—and we would also be healthier and happier.

Think about this: Were you thankful this morning that you could jump out of bed and walk to the bathroom without needing assistance or a walker to get there? If breathing is something you do regularly without any effort, have you thought of what a blessing it is? All we need to do is watch someone who has a severe case of emphysema and has to carry an oxygen tank at all times, and we will be very thankful for the breath we usually take for granted.

> *We would all be surprised by our blessings if we would count them.*

An Amazing Man

Once in a while we encounter someone amazing—someone who lives under circumstances that seem terrible to us. Yet, somehow, that person tells us what they are thankful for and seems to be happier than we are, although we would consider our circumstances much better than theirs.

I once had the pleasure of meeting someone I will never forget. During my first trip to India, we went to a leper colony to feed and encourage the people living there. Leprosy is easily curable, but these people had not been able to obtain or pay for the medicine that would help them. To me the circumstances of the leper village were awful. The disease had eaten away parts of people's bodies.

One man asked me to come and see his home, and he was visibly excited about it. I am not sure what I expected, but certainly not what I saw. His home was a space, perhaps six feet long by four feet wide, dug out of the side of a hill. He had stretched out a hammock for his bed, and in the corner were a few dented pots that looked as though they had been used by someone for many years. That was it! That is what he was so thankful for and excited about.

I still shake my head in disbelief when I think of him, but he is living proof that anyone can be thankful if they truly want to be. He had so little that anything he did have was a reason to celebrate. He saw more wonder in the little dirt hillside hole he called home than most of us do in our "mini mansions," which we complain about having to clean. Yes, if you have a home in the Western world, you have a mansion compared to most of the rest of the world.

The man in my story was thankful, and he said so loudly. Remember, silent gratitude doesn't mean anything to anyone, so "be thankful and say so" (Psalm 100:4 AMPC).

I would like to be one of those amazing people who finds something to be thankful for no matter how many difficulties I face, wouldn't you? Let's agree to make this a top priority in our lives. Someone once told me that his goal is to be the most thankful person on the earth, but he will have to make room for me, because this is now my goal, too.

CHAPTER 5

Grateful for God-Winks

I woke up, I have clothes to wear, I have running water, I have food to eat, life is good, God is great, I'm thankful.

Author Unknown

As I lay in bed one morning several years ago, I thought about people who are unable to simply wake up, get out of bed, and begin their day because they use a wheelchair or have other handicaps that prevent them from doing so. I started thanking God that I could walk, talk, see, and hear—faculties for which I had not thanked Him before. I think we may take these and other abilities for granted, but they are great blessings, and we should thank God for them. In fact, I think we would greatly miss most of the things we do easily, day after day, without giving them much thought, if we were unable to do them.

As that morning went on, I thought of how nice it is to have hot and cold running water in my home, a warm robe to wear when the house is chilly, and a furnace with a thermostat that can easily be adjusted to make my surroundings warmer in a matter of a few minutes. I had coffee to drink in front of my fireplace and plenty of books to read, which reminded me of God's goodness in my life. When the time came to get dressed, I had multiple outfits to choose from and many pairs of shoes. It was barely eight a.m., and I had already found at least one hundred things for which to be thankful, things I normally took for granted simply because they were always available.

Taking our blessings for granted is a mistake, and I believe our joy will increase dramatically if we begin to notice them rather than assume they will always be readily available to us.

Last night the power went out for two hours at our house, causing quite an inconvenience. I immediately started praying that God would move to get it turned back on quickly, but I cannot even remember the last time that I thanked God for all the electricity that flows effortlessly into my home, continuously powering all my electric gadgets and providing light in the darkness. When the power went off, I groped my way through the house, searching for a flashlight or some candles. Yes, I bumped into a few walls and stubbed my toe a couple of times. And I remembered what a blessing electricity is.

The apostle Paul says that we are to always give thanks "for all things to God the Father" (Ephesians 5:20 NKJV). Much of what I noticed that day was included in the "all things" I had taken for granted.

What's a God-Wink?

Perhaps you have never heard the term *God-wink* before and are wondering what it is. That is probably because I made it up—or at least I thought I did, and then I heard it being used on television as a movie title. I wanted to think they got it from me, but a friend told me she had heard the word used for quite a while. Once again, my ego had to take a hit when I found I wasn't as brilliant as I thought I was.

I have been getting winks from God for a good number of years, but for a long time I did not have a name for these experiences. God-winks are the little things that God does for us that may only be meaningful to us, but they let us know that He is present and watching over us. He sees us and He cares about what we call "needs," which are often only wants, but He provides them just because He loves us.

> God-winks are the little things that God does for us that may only be meaningful to us.

I've been married to Dave since 1967, yet it would say something special to me if we were in a crowd and he winked at me from across the room. No words would have to be exchanged, but I would know what that wink meant. It would mean that he loves me, that he notices me, and that I am very important to him.

When God winks at us, it also means that He loves us and notices us and that we are very important to Him. Sadly, we often miss His winks because we write them off as coincidences when perhaps we should see them as miracles. We say we want God to do miracles in our lives. Perhaps He does them all the time and we just don't see them.

God's love is something we can see evidence of if we look for it. We believe we have it by faith and should never judge whether God loves us based on what He does or doesn't do for us. Nevertheless, I do believe quite often that God shows His love to us and we miss it because we are not aware of it or watching for it.

I got a wink from God when I was purchasing an item at a department store and the clerk asked if I had a 40-percent-off coupon. I said, "I don't, but I wish I did." She took time to go find one and cut it out of the advertisement flyer for me. You may call this a coincidence. But I say God just winked at me.

Sometimes, I notice what I call "seasons" of God showing off in my life. In the past week, I have had God-winks almost every day. I wanted to get my hair washed and styled, but when I called, I was told the salon was booked. Then, suddenly the woman said, "Wait a minute. Let me see what I can do." When she returned to the phone, she said, "I worked it out. You can get your hair done now!"

I was also given an unexpected 25 percent off at a shop. They called it a "friends and family discount," but I called it a God-wink. Later, we got the last available table at a restaurant that was packed. My son called just to tell me he loved me, and my other son dropped by with flowers.

God works through people, and even though we should thank them for what they do for us, we should also thank God, because the blessings we receive are actually God working through people to bless and encourage us. The Bible teaches that we have favor with God and that He gives us favor with people (Proverbs 3:4).

We can and should train ourselves to watch for the special ways God helps, encourages, and blesses us and say thank You! We cannot experience the power of thank you unless we practice

> *We cannot experience the power of thank you unless we practice thinking and saying it.*

thinking and saying it. This is a great way to stay focused on God and connected with Him all day, every day. He is never more than a thought or a word of thanks away from us, and He winks at us more often than we may realize. In fact, Scripture tells us that God is with us at all times and promises never to leave us (Deuteronomy 31:8). This is wonderful to know, but we get an extra blessing when we find ways to converse with Him throughout the day. Saying thank You is just one of many ways we can do this.

Focus on the Positive

Focusing on what we have to be thankful for will prevent us from being faultfinders. It seems that human nature apart from God drifts toward negativity if we do not intentionally focus on what is positive. There may be a few people out of the billions on earth who are born with those sunny, bubbly, never-see-a-problem type of personalities, but certainly not most of us. I don't know about you, but I'm not one of them, so I have to train and discipline myself to keep moving in a positive direction and to ask God for a lot of help.

As I write this book, the world is ten months into a pandemic with millions of people who have or have had COVID-19, an illness caused by a virus that spreads from person to person. It has spread throughout the world, and we have had to wear facemasks that cover the mouth and nose when in public and quarantine if exposed to the virus. People have been out of work. Businesses, restaurants, and other places we frequent and depend on have been closed or able to offer only partial service. Many of them have even had to close permanently because of lost revenue. The pandemic has definitely affected millions of people adversely, and maintaining a positive attitude is more challenging than usual. But, even in the midst of times such as these, we have a great deal for which to be thankful.

I truly believe that no matter how bad something may be for us, there is always someone whose circumstances are worse than ours. Although we may have to search harder than usual, we can find good things to focus on. If you stop right now, you can immediately think of a dozen blessings to be thankful for without even making much of an effort. Why not take time to try it?

I can be aggravated that my vision is not as good as it once was, or I can be thankful for contact lenses that allow me to see without wearing glasses. I can be frustrated that I have to take medicine, or I can be thankful that God gave someone the creative ability to make the medicine that helps me. What about you? Is there something you have complained about and allowed to frustrate you that you could look at differently and turn into a thank you?

You may have heard of an old movie called *Pollyanna*. It is about a little girl who has one of those sunny, bubbly, everything-is-wonderful personalities, and she plays what she calls the "glad game." In her game, no matter how bad something is, she turns it into something glad. She invites unhappy people to play her game, but not everyone is willing to join her. As foolish as it seems, some people simply are not willing to be happy. If they aren't, we should not let them make us unhappy.

These sour people usually say that life is difficult and that they refuse to ignore reality by acting joyful. What they are really doing is focusing on the aspects of reality that are negative without seeing the parts that are wonderful. No matter how many bad things or people are in the world, I will always believe that there are more good situations and people than bad ones. The problem in the world is not the bad things; it is that people focus on and highlight the bad without balancing it with the good. God is good, and He is doing good things constantly. We simply need to watch for His goodness.

Lest I be accused of refusing to pay close attention to what is going on in the world and do my part to stand against it and make the world better, let me say that I don't think we should ignore reality. Our world is in serious trouble—not just our world, but more importantly the people in our world—and we should all be responsible for praying and doing whatever God asks us to do to make it better. At the same time, part of what is wrong in the world is that most people only see what is wrong. I encourage all of us, myself included, to focus on and

> *Part of what is wrong in the world is that most people only see what is wrong.*

highlight the good and positive things that God does all the time to let us know that He is here, that He loves us, and that He is still in control. If we watch for His winks, we will see them.

All Things Work Together for Good

Perhaps you have heard Romans 8:28: "All things work together for good to those who love God, to those who are the called according to His purpose" (NKJV). I can testify that even when something we think is terrible happens, it can still work out for our benefit if we will continue believing that God is good and that nothing is impossible with Him. I recently had a couple of experiences that reminded me just how true this scripture is.

Growing up with a sexually abusive father and a mother who abandoned me emotionally caused untold stress on me during my early life. That stress continued through subsequent years as I tried to overcome the damage my soul (mind, will, and emotions) suffered through abuse. Because of this, I have had to take anxiety medicine. My doctor advised me to take it, and as long as I chose not to do so, I continued to struggle with intense tension and headaches.

I refused to take the medicine for a long time for two reasons. One reason was that there is a stigma attached to it in some spiritual circles. The other reason was that my mother had serious mental problems, and I had developed the mistaken idea that anyone who took medicine for anxiety or depression also had mental problems. I was wrong about that. My mother's problems stemmed from not dealing with what my father was doing to me, not from a medical problem. Secrets can make people sick, and that was the case with her.

I finally decided to take the medicine, and sure enough my headaches stopped and I was able to relax.

I also have mild adrenal hyperplasia and a benign tumor on one of my adrenal glands, which causes my hormones to malfunction. My doctor has told me that this condition in itself, without even considering my background, would be sufficient cause to need help.

People who take medicine for emotional issues have been looked down on in the body of Christ for a long time, and I think it is time for that to stop. Our emotions are part of who we are, and they can be damaged or sick, just as a liver or a heart can be. If you tell people you have to take heart medication, they don't think it is odd at all. But if you tell some people you take medicine for anxiety, depression, panic disorder, bipolar depression, obsessive-compulsive disorder, schizophrenia, or other mental or emotional illnesses, many would immediately judge you as someone who simply can't handle life. A large majority of people who need these medicines feel shame about taking them and they shouldn't.

I've written books on emotional healing, and I believe we can be healed emotionally, but sometimes medicine and/or counseling, along with God's Word, is part of that healing. Sometimes these supports are needed only for a short period of time to help a person through a tragedy or an especially difficult time. In fact, within the past few months, two Christian physicians have told me that because of tragic circumstances in their lives, they had to take anxiety medicine for six months and were then able to discontinue it.

According to the Anxiety and Depression Association of America, approximately 40 million Americans over the age of eighteen struggle with anxiety. *Forty million.* This number is rising, and it does not include the number of children and adolescents diagnosed with anxiety issues. Approximately 25 percent of people ages thirteen to seventeen deal with anxiety. This tells me that anxiety is a serious problem in our culture. I hope that those who truly need medication will never be ashamed to take it and that those who can manage their anxiety in other ways will be diligent to do so.

We should never take any kind of medicine unless we truly need it, but if we do need it, we should thank God that it is available. I read about a very well-known minister who suffered terribly with depression for most of his life. He finally decided to take medicine for it, and he says that he now thanks God every morning when he swallows the pill that God used to change his life.

Chances are, too many people who could experience total healing through the application of God's Word probably run to the medicine bottle too quickly. But there are also times when God uses the miracle of medicine and/or counseling along with His Word to help us. No matter how much anxiety medicine a person takes, it cannot replace knowing that God loves us, accepts us, and knows our worth and value in Him. These are the important things, not the medicine, but the medicine may also be a tool that God uses to bring healing.

I recently had a wonderful experience that fits into the principle of all things working together for good. The anxiety medicine I had taken for years suddenly became unavailable. I had no warning of this and no time to prepare for it. The company that made it simply quit producing it. When I heard this, I distinctly remember starting to panic and then thinking, *All things work together for good to those who love God. I love Him, so perhaps this will force me to do something that will help me with some of the side effects of the medicine I have been on.*

Most medicines have side effects. In my case, the medicine caused extremely dry eyes and light sensitivity. In addition, my energy level was lower than I needed it to be. My doctor and I chose a different medicine, and now my dry eyes are much better, the sensitivity to light is better, I am not as tired, and I take less medicine than I did before. In this case, God caused what looked like a problem to be a blessing. I am now very thankful that the manufacturer stopped making the previous medication, because it forced me to make a change that has been good for me. I had been praying for God to heal me from the side effects I mentioned, and He did—just not the way I would have expected.

A Second Blessing

Another similar situation—a big God-wink—occurred about a week later. I had surgery scheduled on my right shoulder due to calcification tendinitis, arthritis, and some minor labral tears. The surgeon rescheduled the procedure twice because of issues related to COVID-19. On both occasions, I had blocked out time for the surgery and recovery on my calendar, and I also had appointments for all the physical therapy sessions that would be needed. Changing my schedule is not easy, so delaying the procedure was quite an ordeal.

Soon after the second cancellation, I was traveling and went into a medical salon for a special type of facial. However, I made a mistake and went on the wrong day. At the reception desk was a doctor who introduced himself to me and said he was familiar with me from watching me on television. As we talked together, I discovered he was known for a procedure that I wanted to try before having surgery, but I had not been able to find anyone who did it. So, the delayed shoulder operation looked like an inconvenience, and going to the medical salon on the wrong day was a mistake. But, it turned out that God was guiding me to what I wanted initially. I ended up having the procedure I originally wanted, and it helped me not to need the surgery.

God-winks? I think I can say, "Yes and amen!" God is winking at you, too, but maybe you just need to open your eyes and see your life from a little different perspective. As you go about each day, be attentive to what happens to you and the blessings that come your way. These things are not random; they are God's ways of getting your attention and adding a bit of happiness and a touch of His love to your everyday life.

CHAPTER 6

Gratitude and Generosity

You have not lived today until you have done something for someone who can never repay you.

John Bunyan

I believe that generosity is one of the most beautiful attitudes in the world. God is generous to us, and when we are generous to others, we show that we are truly thankful for all He does for us. When I receive a blessing, I want to share it with my family or someone who is in need. I certainly was not always this way, and I give God all the credit for making that change in me.

Gratitude, joy, and generosity are a never-ending cycle. When I am thankful, it makes me feel happy, and when I am thankful and happy, it makes me want to give. Then, when I give, I'm even happier, which makes me even more thankful.

You don't have to wait for something good to happen to you before you start being generous. You can start the cycle in your life by taking one step of generosity. When you do, you will experience the benefits of it. Jesus says, "It is more blessed to give than to receive" (Acts 20:35), and I believe this wholeheartedly.

The scientific community has studied the effects of being grateful for the past two decades, and they have discovered its value and benefits. Being thankful makes us happier, promotes better sleep, keeps us healthier, and makes us more generous. I have even heard that scientists can watch a scan of the brain function when people express thankfulness, and it shows definite changes taking place in the frontal lobe. It turns out that there is a deep neural connection between gratitude and giving.

A Short Lesson on Gratitude and Generosity

This is a powerful story on the fact that thankfulness inspires generosity.

A blind boy sat on the steps of a building with a hat by his feet. He held up a sign which read, "I am blind, please help."

There were only a few coins in the hat—spare change from folks as they hurried past. A man was walking by. He took a few coins from his pocket and dropped them into the hat. He then took the sign, turned it around, and wrote some words. Then he put the sign back in the boy's hand so that everyone who walked by would see the new words.

Soon the hat began to fill up. A lot more people were giving money to the blind boy. That afternoon, the man who had changed the sign returned to see how things were. The boy recognized his footsteps and asked, "Were you the one who changed my sign this morning? What did you write?"

The man said, "I only wrote the truth. I said what you said but in a different way. I wrote, 'Today is a beautiful day, but I cannot see it.'"

Both signs spoke the truth. But the first sign simply said the boy was blind, while the second sign conveyed to everyone walking by how grateful they should be to see.[5]

We see from this story that when the people walking by were inspired, they wanted to be generous.

Thankful People Want to Give

The New Testament story of Zacchaeus also teaches that when we are grateful, we become generous (Luke 19:1–9). Zacchaeus was a tax collector, and in those days tax collectors were among the most hated people in society because they were usually dishonest. They collected the taxes due to the government but were also allowed to collect monies they wanted for themselves. You can imagine how greedy some of them were.

Apparently, Zacchaeus was tired of the way he was living, because when he heard that Jesus was passing by, he was determined to see Him. Because Zacchaeus was short in stature and unable to see Jesus over all the people who had gathered, he ran ahead of the crowd and climbed up in a tree so that when Jesus walked by, he could easily see Him.

As Jesus passed under the tree where Zacchaeus sat, He looked up and told him to come down because He was going to his house. "Zacchaeus stood up and said to the Lord, 'Look, Lord! Here and now I give half of my possessions to the poor, and if I have cheated anybody out of anything, I will pay back four times the amount'" (Luke 19:8). Jesus then said, "Today salvation has come to this house" (Luke 19:9).

Zacchaeus was so thankful to have Jesus

come to his home and forgive his sins that, without any prompting from anyone, he immediately wanted to be generous.

I want to mention two more stories in the Bible that demonstrate the principle that gratitude leads to generosity: the story of Esther and the story of Nehemiah.

Esther

Esther, whose story is in the biblical book that bears her name, was a young Jewish woman called by God to save an entire nation of Jews who were scheduled to be killed by a wicked man named Haman. Haman had deceived the king, causing him to believe the Jews deserved to die, but they didn't. Esther was to enter the king's harem, where she hoped to be allowed into the king's presence so she could ask for the deliverance of her people. In order for this to happen, she had to have great favor with the king. The king had met Esther and did admire her, but in the culture of Esther's time, she was not allowed to go before him without an invitation; otherwise she could be killed.

As the time for the killing of the Jews drew

near, Esther knew she had to make a move, even if it cost her her life. She fasted and prayed and went before the king. In his presence, the only way she would know she was safe would be for him to extend to her his golden scepter. He did hold out the scepter, and Esther invited him to a banquet in his honor. The king accepted the invitation, and during the banquet she was able to present her petition to him. Because he granted her desire, the Jews were saved, and Haman was hanged for his treachery. Esther's uncle, Mordecai, who had originally asked Esther to intervene with the king on behalf of the Jews, was honored and given authority in the land.

A letter was sent to the Jews throughout the land, instructing them to celebrate annually the fourteenth and fifteenth days of the month of Adar as the days the Jews found relief from their enemies and as the month when their sorrow was turned into joy. They were also told to give presents of food to one another and gifts to the poor (Esther

> *Giving to others was one way the Israelites celebrated and showed their thanks for what God had done for them.*

9:19–22). We see that their gratitude turned into generosity. Giving to others was one way the Israelites celebrated and showed their thanks for what God had done for them.

Nehemiah

The biblical account of Nehemiah took place at a time when Jerusalem's walls protecting the Jewish people were broken down. Nehemiah, who worked as a cupbearer for the king of Persia, requested permission to rebuild it. The story of the rebuilding is lengthy, but let me simply say that the king did grant Nehemiah permission to lead the rebuilding of the wall, and it was no easy task. Nehemiah and those who helped him had to fight enemies continually to accomplish the job.

When the wall was finished, everyone rejoiced. The people's participation in the dedication ceremony involved the bringing of tithes, contributions, and firstfruits offerings to God's storehouse, so there would be provision for the people in the days to come (Nehemiah 10:35–39). You can read the Book of Nehemiah to get the entire story.

I find it interesting that one way God instructed His people to celebrate their victories under the Old Covenant—in Nehemiah's and Esther's stories, among others—was to give to others. If they were generous under the law (in Old Testament times), how much more generous should we be now that we live under the grace of God through our Lord Jesus Christ? How can we not be thankful for and celebrate with generosity the wonderful things that God has done for us?

Great People of the Bible and Their Generosity

I believe all truly great men and women are thankful, generous people. Consider these remarkable men and women whose stories are included in Scripture.

Abraham

Abraham was generous to Lot in giving him the best part of the land when their herdsmen were arguing (Genesis 13:5–12).

Joseph

Joseph was generous to his brothers who had sorely mistreated him; he freely forgave them and provided for them during a famine. His words are too beautiful not to share them in this book:

> His brothers then came and threw themselves down before him. "We are your slaves," they said. But Joseph said to them, "Don't be afraid. Am I in the place of God? You intended to harm me, but God intended it for good to accomplish what is now being done, the saving of many lives. So then, don't be afraid. I will provide for you and your children." And he reassured them and spoke kindly to them.
>
> Genesis 50:18–21

You may remember that Joseph's brothers had sold him into slavery and told their father he had been killed. He continued to experience injustices everywhere he went and even spent thirteen years in prison for a crime he did not commit. But God was with him and continued to give him favor. With the favor, promotion, and authority that God gave him, he could have easily taken revenge on his brothers. However, I am sure he was very thankful for all God had brought him through and for the ways God promoted him, so he responded to the evil done to him with generosity, not revenge.

Job

I have written about Job already, but let me remind you that he was the most righteous person in the land. Although God dealt with him about his self-righteousness, he did treat others very well by helping the poor and the fatherless (Job 1:8; 29:12). Speaking of himself, Job said these remarkable words:

> If I have withheld from the poor and needy what they desired, or have caused the eyes of the widow to look in vain [for relief], or have eaten my morsel alone and have not shared it with the fatherless—no, but from my youth [the fatherless] grew up with me as a father, and I have been [the widow's] guide from my mother's womb—if I have

seen anyone perish for want of clothing, or any poor person without covering, if his loins have not blessed me [for clothing them], and if he was not warmed with the fleece of my sheep, if I have lifted my hand against the fatherless when I saw [that the judges would be favorable and be] my help at the [council] gate, then let my shoulder fall away from my shoulder blade, and my arm be broken from its socket.

Job 31:16–22 AMPC

I find these scriptures to be very moving and powerful. Job said in essence that if he didn't use his arm to help the needy, it should be torn from his body. I think this shows how important it is to be generous to those in need.

Mary Magdalene, Joanna, and Susanna

Luke's gospel mentions three women who extended generosity to Jesus: Joanna, Susanna, and Mary Magdalene. They helped support Jesus and His disciples in their ministry "out of their own means" (Luke 8:3). This is the same Mary Magdalene out of whom Jesus had cast seven demons (Luke 8:2), and we can only imagine how thankful she was for her freedom from torment. I am sure that her generosity was a reflection of her gratitude.

I have read that Jesus talked more about money than He spoke about heaven or hell. Why? Because the way we use our money says a lot about how thankful we are for the life we have. A stingy person cannot possibly be a thankful one, because the more thankful we are, the more generous we will be. We won't have to be talked into generosity or forced to be generous in any way; we will extend it cheerfully, as God desires.

> The way we use our money says a lot about how thankful we are for the life we have.

Paul told the Corinthians not to give under compulsion, but to give cheerfully because God loves a cheerful giver.

The point is this: whoever sows sparingly will also reap sparingly, and whoever sows bountifully will also reap bountifully. Each one must give as he has decided in his

heart, not reluctantly or under compulsion,
for God loves a cheerful giver.
                    2 Corinthians 9:6–7 ESV

Helen Keller said, "There is no better way to thank God for your sight than by giving a helping hand to someone in the dark." She was talking about being thankful for physical eyesight, but what about the light God has brought into our lives spiritually? Are we thankful for salvation through Christ, the unconditional love of God, and His promise to never leave us? Are we grateful for what God has done and continues to do moment by moment? If we are indeed thankful, the proof will be seen in our generosity.

The greatest act of generosity the world has ever seen was when God gave His only Son because of His love for us (see John 3:16). His actions teach us to give generously.

The Thank Offering

Under the Old Testament Law of Moses, God's people were instructed to bring thank offerings at various times. I will share only one place in

Scripture that speaks of the thank offering, but the Bible includes multiple references to it.

> If he offers it by way of thanksgiving, then along with the sacrifice of thanksgiving he shall offer unleavened cakes mixed with oil, and unleavened wafers spread with oil, and cakes of well stirred fine flour mixed with oil. With the sacrifice of his peace offerings for thanksgiving, he shall present his offering with cakes of leavened bread.
>
> Leviticus 7:12–13 NASB

We no longer live under the Law of Moses, but the spirit of the law should still be respected. The Old Testament gives us many good examples we can follow because we want to, not because we have to. I like to occasionally give a special "thank offering"—something beyond my regular giving—simply to say, "Thank You, Father, for all You have done for me."

This is not required, of course, but I share it as a suggestion to draw your attention to all God has done for you and a way to thank Him for it.

I set aside a specified sum of money each month to give to various people who have a financial need or who simply need a blessing. We can all give gifts—even a five-dollar gift card for a cup of coffee—as a way of encouraging people or even as a way to say thank you to them. They are blessed by the gifts, and the giving makes us happy.

How do you view your giving? Do you see it as an obligation or a privilege? Do you give merely because you have a habit of doing so, or do you give from a heart of true gratitude for all God has done for you? Winston Churchill said, "We make a living by what we get, but we make a life by what we give."

> Do you see your giving as an obligation or a privilege?

CHAPTER 7

Never Forget Where You Came From

Count your blessings and give God praise for the great and wonderful things he has done, for what He is doing right now and for the great things he has in store for you in the future.

Bob Richardson

Everything that happens to us is part of our story, and, as believers, *all* things work together for our good (Romans 8:28). You may have been through something difficult and despised it while you were going through it, but now you see that it made you a better person. Everything can be used for a purpose if we give it to God.

A good example of how everything works together for good is baking a cake. Some of the ingredients served by themselves wouldn't be tasty or enjoyable. Think about putting a few spoonfuls of plain flour into your mouth or drinking one-half cup of oil or eating a raw egg. That all sounds disgusting, but when they are blended together with a few other items and baked, you get a delicious cake.

This is one way we can look at our life. God takes the difficulties and mixes them with blessings, and somehow it all works out well in the end. Truly believing that all things work together for our good helps me to remain hopeful and positive through hardship and suffering, and I know it will help you, too.

First Corinthians 10:13 promises that God will never allow more to come on us than we can endure, and that He always provides the way out. At times we go through seasons of trials and difficulties, and we can easily begin to think that we just can't take any more. When those thoughts come, it is good to rely on 1 Corinthians 10:13 and remember that God will not allow circumstances to break us and will always provide a way of escape from temptation.

God tells us to forget and let go of the past, yet He also tells us not to forget where we came from and all that He has done for us. Deuteronomy 8 is a powerful chapter in the Bible, and I recommend that you read all of it. In it, God reminds the Israelites of the time they spent in the wilderness, where He humbled them and tested them to see whether they would keep His commands or not. He goes on to tell them that He humbled and tested them so He could bring them into a good land that lacked nothing. And then He warned them not to forget Him and all He had done for them. Although they did not have everything they wanted, God provided everything they needed. Then He said this:

> Be careful that you do not forget the Lord your God, failing to observe his commands, his laws and his decrees that I am giving you this day. Otherwise, when you eat and are satisfied, when you build fine houses and settle down, and when your herds and flocks grow large and your silver and gold increase and all you have is multiplied, then your heart will become proud and you will forget the Lord your God, who brought you out of Egypt, out of the land of slavery.
>
> Deuteronomy 8:11–14

God had a great future prepared for His people, but He had to prepare them for all the good He wanted to give them. Quite often we think we are ready to handle the things we ask God to give us. We don't understand the delays when He doesn't seem to be moving us in the direction in which we desire to go, but He is doing in us a work that needs to be done before we get what we want. Let's remember and believe that God's timing is always perfect.

Soon after God called me to teach His Word, I wanted and prayed for a large ministry. I wanted to help people all over the world, but God gave me only small things to do. This was frustrating to me, because I had such big dreams in my heart. The large vision God gave me was indeed His will, but I didn't realize that it would come in due time, when I could handle all the responsibilities of the type of ministry I hoped to have. When I first prayed for a big ministry, I wasn't mature enough spiritually to represent God to the very large audiences to whom I wanted to minister.

The ministry grew gradually, and all the while God was changing me little by little. If you have a big dream and it seems slow in coming, don't be discouraged. Keep pressing on and cooperate with the work the Holy Spirit is doing as He prepares you for the fulfillment of your dreams. Be thankful each step of the way and remember that people who are faithful over a little will eventually be made rulers over much (Matthew 25:23).

Moral Decline

The United States of America was once known for its pulpits, which were aflame with righteousness. It was common to hear people talking about God on a regular basis, and most people went to church on Sundays to worship Him. But our culture has changed, and not for the better. The United States' national debt is astronomical, our world standing in education has slipped drastically, creativity is disappearing, and other nations no longer respect us as they once did.

The decline we have seen in America, I believe, is because we are guilty of doing what God warned the Israelites not to do. We have forgotten God and are no longer thankful for His miraculous acts. We take for granted blessings such as the tremendous prosperity we enjoy as a nation, the inventions that have helped our country and the world, the gift of religious freedom, and the opportunity for anyone to build a wonderful life through hard work and diligence.

In order to keep our blessings, we must keep God first in our lives. Sadly, there is currently a movement to remove God from every sector of society, and we are even seeing the persecution of Christians. Morality is at an all-time low, and integrity and honor seem to be things of the past. Thankfully, there is a remnant of people who love God with all their heart and who strive to live godly lives. I am glad for that, but I want godliness and love for God to characterize the majority of people as they once did and as I believe they can again.

True repentance and thankfulness to God from our government officials and all citizens could turn our situation around very quickly. We do not have a money problem in America; we have a moral problem. If America will lift up God and give Him the place He deserves in our society, our nation can be healed.

The prosperity with which we have been blessed as a nation should make us tremendously thankful, yet it seems to have the opposite effect on many people. They believe that they are self-sufficient and forget the God who helped them prosper in the first place.

It seems to me that the more convenience we have, the softer we become. We become upset about minor inconveniences, and we can be impatient and lacking in endurance. I remember when people were tougher; they had more stamina and didn't cave in at the first sign of trouble. If we want to have and enjoy just about every blessing anyone could think of, the very least we can do is be thankful for them. Remembering what life was like without them helps us do that.

In Deuteronomy 8:17–19, God warned the Israelites against saying in their hearts and minds that their own strength had gotten them the wealth they had. He further warned them that if they did, they would perish.

> God's goodness provides our blessings, and being thankful for those blessings allows us to keep them.

God's goodness provides our blessings, and being thankful for those blessings allows us to keep them.

It is important for us to stand firm in doing what we know to be right. This is one way we can say thank you to the Lord for His goodness. Even if everyone you know compromises their Christian morality, I encourage you to stand firm in righteous behavior. Then, if conditions in the world do get worse, God will be able to protect you. God protected Noah during a flood, He protected the children of Israel when the angel of death passed over, and He protected Joseph during a famine.

Each of us is responsible for our own decisions and behavior, and we can never excuse compromise by saying, "It is okay to compromise because everyone does it." We are not to be like everyone else; we are called to be bright lights representing Jesus in a dark world. Many people are searching for answers, and we can be an example to them if we will boldly walk with God no matter what others choose to do. We should always be growing in godly character and never be in decline.

Don't Steal the Glory That Belongs to God

God has said that He will not yield His glory to another (Isaiah 42:8), and this is one reason we should voice our thankfulness to God frequently. We cannot say thank you too often. The more thankful we are and the more often we express our gratitude, the more it shows our humility. Let me remind you that a humble person will always be a thankful person.

> A humble person will always be a thankful person.

Daniel 4 is another place in the Bible that reminds us of the dangers of pride and the wisdom of humility. In this story, God was blessing King Nebuchadnezzar greatly. In the first four verses of the chapter, the king said it was his pleasure to tell the people about the miraculous signs and wonders God had performed for him. Verse 4 says he was contented, prosperous, and at rest in his palace. Notice that as long as the king gave God the glory for his blessings, he was prosperous and at rest. But by verse 30 of chapter 4 he had declined and was bragging about the great city he had built by his power and majesty of his own hand. While the words were still in his mouth, God stripped him of his kingdom, and he lived in the wilderness as a wild beast for seven years (vv. 31–33). Then his sanity was restored, and he praised God once again (vv. 34–35). All the king had lost was restored, and he said of God, "Everything he does is right and all his ways are just. And those who walk in pride he is able to humble" (v. 37).

> God gives us an opportunity to humble ourselves, but if we don't, He will do it for us.

God gives us an opportunity to humble ourselves, but if we don't, He will do it for us.

Looking Back

Dave and I enjoy reflecting on how far God has brought us since the early days of our ministry.

It began in the basement of our home, which we turned into offices. We had about eight employees, all working in our house. Our first employee used a cardboard furniture box as a desk. We worked out of that space for about three years, and then we had enough money to rent 1,700 square feet in an office complex. We were so thankful for that space!

Now we have an amazing building, plus a distribution center, totaling 218,000 square feet, and it is all debt-free. I'm amazed and thankful for our ministry headquarters each time I go up the driveway to my office or the television studio. I want to always remember where I came from and stay amazed at what God has done.

I've lived long enough to have done without conveniences such as dishwashers, escalators, air-conditioning, and heat at the flip of a switch. In addition to other stories I have shared in this book about my childhood, I also remember as a young girl having to go outside and down two flights of stairs in the cold winter to the furnace room in the basement, where I shoveled coal out of a coal bin into the furnace so the fire would not go out. This had to be done a few times a day.

We did not have a television until I was about

ten years old. At that time, there were three channels, and we surely couldn't sit in a chair and change channels with a remote control, as we can today. When I was an adolescent, our phone was a three-way party line, which meant that we often had to wait for other people to finish their calls before we could make ours. There were no computers or cell phones until I was about forty years old, and now, we become panic-stricken if a cell tower in our area goes out for five minutes.

When I was in my twenties, my car had no power steering, no power windows, and no power brakes. It did not have automatic signals to let people behind me know if I was turning left, right, slowing down, or stopping. In those days, we had to roll down the window (summer and winter) and give hand signals. My car had a stick shift, which meant that I had to shift and use the clutch, as well as give hand signals. Now, the car we have will park itself if we tell it to. Progress is amazing as long as we stay thankful for it. People invent technology that makes our lives easier, but God is always the One who gives them the ability to think and innovate. It is

> *Progress is amazing as long as we stay thankful for it.*

good to admire people, but we should never give them the glory that belongs to God alone.

We didn't go on vacations when I was a young girl because there was no money for that kind of recreation or leisure. I had eight outfits in my closet and two pairs of shoes, so getting dressed was not confusing. I had one outfit for Monday, one for Tuesday, and so on throughout the week. Now, we can easily get stressed trying to figure out the perfect outfit for each day, and although our closets are crammed full, we think, *I have nothing to wear.* Our real problem is choice overload. We have so much that life becomes confusing and sometimes overwhelming.

When I was young, a Popsicle cost five cents. My mom and I divided one every Friday night, and we were thankful and excited when we got it. Eating out was not something people did much at all. I wasn't continually entertained as children today expect to be. I went to school, went home, did homework, did chores, and ate dinner. Once we had a television set, I may have watched one or two thirty-minute shows before going to bed. That same routine repeated itself Monday through Friday, and on weekends I worked as a babysitter or helped my mother clean house.

My entertainment was infrequent and consisted of playing outside or playing card games with a neighbor. We went to visit my grandparents, who lived about two hundred miles away from us, three or four times a year, and we occasionally went on a picnic. Now, some people get depressed if they can't take an expensive vacation at least once or twice each year, and they eat in restaurants frequently.

The world was a fairly nice place when I was younger. Generally speaking, people had good manners, they helped each other, and life was simple. My life wasn't simple because of the sexual abuse, but life in general was simple, and I think people enjoyed it then more than most enjoy it now.

I heard a story about a missionary couple from Africa. When they came to visit the United States, they wanted to get some cereal, because where they lived people could only get one type of cereal, called Weetabix. The husband drove his wife to the store, and she went inside. After about forty-five minutes, she returned to the car with nothing. "Where's the cereal?" he asked.

She replied, "They have so many different kinds that I became confused and couldn't make a decision."

We have a problem
when what should be
a blessing becomes
a frustration.

I think we can all relate to her experience and have dealt with similar frustrations at times. We have a problem when what should be a blessing becomes a frustration.

I'm sure you have stories of your own—things you can remember that will make you thankful for what you have now. If you haven't thought of them for a while, maybe it is time you do. When you consider how much easier certain tasks are now than they once were, you will appreciate conveniences you may often overlook.

Spiritual Blessings

I could write on and on about modern conveniences and material blessings I enjoy now because I didn't always have them, but my spiritual blessings are far more important and precious to me than anything in this world.

I am thankful for peace, because there were many years in my life when I didn't even know what peace felt like. When Dave and I first married, our relationship involved much turmoil, and most of it was my fault. The only way I knew how to get what I wanted was to argue and become angry. I worried and was frustrated most of the time. I thank God that, through Dave's example of staying calm and peaceful, I finally became so hungry for peace that I was willing to let God teach me His ways of handling situations and people. When I first started to feel peace, it seemed almost boring to me because I was accustomed to living in constant turbulence.

I am so thankful for the peace I enjoy in my life now. When anything happens that even begins to upset me, the first thing I do is pray about it and ask God to solve it and to help me stay calm.

I am thankful to know that through faith in Jesus, God views me as being in right standing with Him (2 Corinthians 5:21). I spent half of my life trying to figure out what was wrong with me. I compared myself with others and always felt as though I fell short of what I should be. I suffered horribly with guilt that was birthed in me during my years of sexual abuse, but God has delivered me from it all. Although I know I am not perfect in all my behavior, I do know that God loves and accepts me. I am free from guilt, wondering what is wrong with me, comparing

myself with other people, and many other negative situations and feelings.

In addition, I am thankful for Jesus, who
paid for all our sins and justified us by His blood
(Romans 3:24–25). I am also thankful for the
Holy Spirit, whom Jesus sent to be with us and
live in us when He ascended to His Father's
right hand (John 14:16–17). You can read more
about God the Father, Jesus, and the Holy Spirit
and the blessings they bring to our lives in chapter 10.

All I need to do is take a little time to remember where I came from spiritually, and I am
immediately thankful. I am sure you are, too.
Let me ask you: What has God delivered you
from? Take some time to think about what your
life was like without Jesus in it. This will help you
overcome any unhappiness you might be having
right now due to imperfect circumstances.

Thank you has power in it.
It helps to keep you full of joy
even when you have good reason to be sad. It is also conta-
gious. When we are thankful and say so, we set
a good example for others to follow.

> Thank you *has power in it.*

The In-Between

The opening quote in this chapter says we should be thankful for the "small things, big things, and everything in between." Joyce Meyer Ministries started very small and now is very large, but there was a lot of in-between. The beginning was exciting. It was new, and we were full of vision. The place we are now is also wonderful, because our dreams have become realities. But the middle, the in-between, wasn't always exciting. As a matter of fact, it was often very difficult. I didn't always give thanks for those times, but I should have, because God used them all to help us get to where we are now.

We often forget to be thankful for things that we have all the time, and we tend to take them for granted. In the movie *Cast Away*, Tom Hanks's character was shipwrecked and lived on an island alone for four years. He had to learn to make do with what he could find on the island, which wasn't

> *We often forget to be thankful for things that we have all the time, and we tend to take them for granted.*

much. He found a volleyball and put a smiley face on it, and it became his best friend. He talked to his new friend about everything. He named his friend Wilson because it was a Wilson Sporting Goods brand volleyball. Maybe the next time we find ourselves complaining about our friends, we should be thankful that we don't have just a volleyball for a friend!

After he was rescued and returned to society, he lay in bed one night and simply flipped the light switch on and off for a long time, soaking in the amazement of being able to do it. I am sure he would have never been amazed by a light switch had he not done without electricity for four years. There are so many little things (not that anything God does is "little") that we expect to be available at all times, and maybe one of the best ways to keep them is to express gratitude for them.

I probably have at least five hundred books in my home. I have heard that when our ministry translates a book into a language from a developing nation, the people in that country sometimes have so little material to help them grow in their faith that they tear the books into chapters and share them. This way, each person has one chapter, so there is enough for everyone to have something. They may be more thankful for their few pages than I am for all my books.

I am thankful today for God and all He has done in my life. Hopefully you are thankful for Him and all He has done in your life, too. Let's make an effort to stay that way every day, no matter what our circumstances may be.

CHAPTER 8

God Doesn't Answer Complaints

The truly patient man neither complains of his hard lot nor desires to be pitied by others. He speaks of his sufferings in a natural, true, and sincere way, without murmuring, complaining, or exaggerating them.

St. Francis de Sales

God answers prayer, but He doesn't answer complaints. One morning, I was spending my usual morning time with Him, and I was focused on all my problems. The Lord spoke to my heart and said, "Joyce, are you going to have fellowship with Me or with your problems this morning?" I was wasting time that could have been used for prayer by murmuring about and focusing on everything I thought was wrong in my life when I should have been focusing on all the ways God has blessed me and praying about my problems with thanksgiving for all of the good things He has done for me.

Pray with Thanksgiving

God delights in answering our prayers, and prayer is one of our greatest privileges. It is not an obligation, but an amazing honor. Instead of complaining as our first response to a problem, we should immediately pray. Complaints open a door for the devil to work in our lives, but prayer with thanksgiving opens a door for God to work

> Complaints open a door for the devil to work in our lives, but prayer with thanksgiving opens a door for God.

in our lives. We know this because Scripture teaches us that the kind of prayer God answers is the kind that is offered with thanksgiving. Consider these verses:

Do not be anxious about anything, but in every situation, by prayer and petition, *with thanksgiving*, present your requests to God. And the peace of God, which transcends all understanding, will guard your hearts and your minds in Christ Jesus.

Philippians 4:6–7 (emphasis mine)

Devote yourselves to prayer, being watchful and *thankful*.

Colossians 4:2 (emphasis mine)

Let the peace of Christ rule in your hearts, since as members of one body you were called to peace. And be *thankful*. Let the message of Christ dwell among you richly as you teach and admonish one another with all wisdom through psalms, hymns, and songs from the Spirit, singing to God *with gratitude* in your hearts. And whatever you do, whether in word or deed, do it all in the name of the Lord Jesus, *giving thanks* to God the Father through him.

Colossians 3:15–17 (emphasis mine)

Rejoice always, pray continually, *give thanks* in all circumstances; for this is God's will for you in Christ Jesus.

1 Thessalonians 5:16–18 (emphasis mine)

Praying with thanksgiving doesn't simply mean thanking God during the prayer but praying from the platform of a thankful life. If we grumble and complain all week and then suddenly want to pray that God will help us with a problem that arises, we may find ourselves not getting the help we desire. God is merciful, and He frequently helps us even though we don't deserve it, but we do need to realize that complaining is dangerous and that it is offensive to Him.

> Praying with thanksgiving means praying from the platform of a thankful life.

Asking God for what we want without thanking Him for what we have reveals a heart that is not right before Him, perhaps a selfish or greedy heart. A heart without gratitude is very unattractive to God.

Ask

The apostle James writes, "You do not have because you do not ask God" (James 4:2). This statement is so simple yet very powerful. We often frustrate ourselves trying to make something happen in our own strength and ability, and we fail to simply ask God for what we want or need. But, when we do make requests of Him, we need to ask in the right way, with the right attitude in our heart.

Scripture tells us to enter His gates with thanksgiving and come into His courts with praise (Psalm 100:4). When we come into God's presence to ask Him anything, we should always come with thanksgiving. To come into His presence with praise is to declare His goodness, magnify His name, and boast, rave about, and

> *When we come into God's presence to ask Him anything, we should always come with thanksgiving.*

speak well of Him. Every time we say that God is good, we are giving Him praise. It is important for us to talk about God's goodness as often as we can and to thank Him for all He has done, is doing, and will do in our lives.

In John 14–16 we are told seven times to ask (14:13, 14; 15:7, 16; 16:23, 24, 26). We can speak to God reverently, yet also as a friend. When we pray, we don't have to try to sound spiritual or be in a certain posture; we simply need to be sincere.

Just think for a few minutes about the amazing privilege of being able to go to the God who created and maintains all things—the God who loves you—and simply ask for His help and tell Him what you want or need. If your request is in accordance with His Word, you can be assured that at just the right time and in the perfect way He will answer your prayer.

Murmuring, Grumbling, Faultfinding, and Complaining

Some businesses have a complaint department, but heaven does not have one. God's Word tells us to do all things without complaining.

Do all things without grumbling and faultfinding and complaining [against God]
and questioning and doubting [among
yourselves].

Philippians 2:14 AMPC

I love the amplification of this scripture,
which says that when we grumble, find fault, and
complain, we are doing it "against God." People
might say right away, "Oh no, Joyce, I am not
complaining against God." Well, He obviously
considers that we are. On one hand, we say we
believe God is in control, but then we murmur
and complain about many things that happen
to us. I am not saying everything that happens,
especially the bad situations or experiences, are
designed by God, but if we remain thankful and
keep a good attitude, He will work them out
for good. Complaining is a
total waste of time and does
no good at all. Complaining
has never solved one of my
problems or yours.

> Complaining is
> a total waste of
> time.

Remaining thankful during difficulty is one
way of waging effective spiritual warfare. When
our enemy, Satan, attacks, he expects us to com-

plain and focus on our problems instead of focusing on God and giving thanks to Him. But we can defeat the enemy by doing the opposite of what he expects. No wonder God says we should give thanks at all times in all things (Ephesians 5:20).

Can you make it through inconveniences and interruptions without complaining? Complaining is a reactionary response to something we don't like. Giving thanks instead of complaining is something we have to do on purpose.

I once decided to keep a record of unpleasant things that happened to me for eight weeks, and here it is:

- I injured my back at the gym.
- Water leaked out of my humidifier and bubbled the wood on my table.
- I broke a nail and had to get it repaired.
- I twisted my wrist and it really hurt.
- I left some luggage on the plane.
- The nursing home called about my mom two times within a few days.
- My back was still hurting, and I hurt my arm doing stretches for my back.
- I spilled a red vitamin drink on a white couch.

- Dave hit a golf ball through a window in a house on the golf course.
- I talked to a pillow in the middle of the night thinking it was Dave.
- I had to spend money I didn't plan to spend replacing a couch I didn't plan to replace.
- Got my little toe caught in my underwear and strained the tendon. It got black and blue and was very swollen and painful.
- I had to tell my very independent eighty-six-year-old aunt that she couldn't drive anymore.
- I had to replace my mother's television so she could have television ears to be able to hear because she would not wear the hearing aids I had already bought her.
- I lost my pants at the spa!
- My mother lost her new $350 glasses. We think she dropped them into the trash can beside her bed.
- Our water was off for twenty-four hours.
- My aunt had shingles in her eyes and had to go to an eye specialist. Because I took care of her and my mom, who are both now deceased, I had to arrange for all doctor visits.

- I had to deal with an unexpected employee situation at work.
- Dave had back surgery and could not go to Indonesia with me.
- Within seven days, I flew forty-seven hours to Indonesia and back, and the city flooded while we were there.
- My aunt was taken to the hospital with pneumonia.
- Three hours after getting home from Indonesia, I got a call to pick up my aunt from the hospital.
- I had a stomach virus after returning from Indonesia.
- I had another employee issue that was rather tense.
- The internet at our office was down for two days.
- Our office phones went down after the internet was fixed.
- I jammed my toe into the leg of the couch.
- I spilled a new box of crackers on the pantry floor and made a big mess.
- I had to tell my aunt she had to move to the nursing home instead of staying in her assisted-living apartment.

- The fire alarms were being tested all day in a hotel where I was staying.
- I drank my entire protein shake and it tasted funny. I later realized that Dave had coated the shaker cup with dishwashing soap the night before to let it soak. I was forever blowing bubbles.

This list indicates approximately one unpleasant situation every other day. You may have a similar list of situations that challenge your thankfulness. Stuff happens! I would love to be able to tell you that I remained thankful throughout the eight weeks, but I am very sure that I didn't. I didn't feel thankful because I was focused on all the annoying things that happened.

When we don't *feel* thankful, we are told to continually offer up a sacrifice of praise to God (Hebrews 13:15). The Israelites had to offer dead animals and food items as sacrifices to God, but under the New Covenant, we get to offer a sacrifice of praise. Even though it is hard at times, it is much easier than what they had to do. And no matter how many annoying problems we have, God is still good, and we are still blessed beyond understanding.

Complaining Is a Sin

The apostle Paul writes that whatever is not of faith is sin (Romans 14:23), and I doubt that we ever complain by faith.

The Book of Numbers gives us insight into how the Israelites thought and behaved as they traveled through the wilderness. They murmured, were impatient, complained, blamed Moses and even God for their problems, and said they just wanted to die (Numbers 21:5).

The New Testament recounts what the Israelites did, and Paul says their story is written "as an example and warning to us" (1 Corinthians 10:11 AMPC). Paul says, "We should not tempt the Lord [try His patience, become a trial to Him, critically appraise Him, and exploit His goodness] as some of them did—and were killed by poisonous serpents" (1 Corinthians 10:9 AMPC).

Complaining prevented many Israelites from entering the Promised Land. Perhaps we should think about this a little more deeply and consider whether our complaining is keeping us from some of the blessings God wants to give us.

Don't Have a Complaint
without a Vision

Do not complain about things you are not willing to do anything about.

Do not complain about things you are not willing to do anything about. Do you complain about your schedule and how busy you are? You must remember that you make your schedule, and you are the only one who can change it. When you think about your schedule, of course, you may immediately think of everything people expect you to do, but God never tells us to try to meet everyone's expectations. We are not to be people-pleasers, but to be God-pleasers. There are many things we could say no to if we were not trying so hard to be popular with other people. God gives us wisdom, and He expects us to use it. If we don't, we will reap the consequences of being foolish. We often say yes when we know in our hearts that we should say no, and that certainly is not wise.

Do you complain about being tired most of the time? The solution is to get more sleep or rest, but in order to do so you may have to give up some things you want to do because they prevent you from getting the rest and sleep you need.

Are you complaining about being in debt? The answer is to stop buying items you could do without, and then systematically pay off the debt you have. Sure, you will have to do without some things, perhaps for a long while, in order to reach this goal, but complaining about it while doing nothing to change it is useless.

We have countless decisions to make, and we need to prioritize them. Say yes to the ones you know are important, and when your schedule is comfortably full, start saying no. Your health is more important than keeping all your friends happy with you. It is important enough that you should say no even to things you would really like to do if doing them means you will get no rest or put too much stress on yourself.

God should always come first, then your family, then taking care of yourself, and then everything else. You may wonder if making a high priority of taking care of yourself is selfish. The answer is, no, it isn't. If you don't take care of yourself, then you won't have any energy to give to anyone else.

Complaints are nothing new. People throughout history have complained, but many of them turned their complaints into positive action. For example:

- Nehemiah had a complaint about the broken-down walls of his city, but instead of simply complaining about it, he told the king about his vision to rebuild the wall and asked for permission to do it (Nehemiah 2:1–8).
- Habakkuk went to God with a complaint, and He responded, "Write the vision and engrave it so plainly upon tablets that everyone who passes may [be able to] read [it easily and quickly]" (Habakkuk 2:2 AMPC).
- Martin Luther King Jr. had a complaint about racism, and he had a vision to end it.
- Nelson Mandela had a complaint about apartheid, but he also had a vision to stop it.

> *If you don't like something, do something about it.*

If you don't like something, do something about it. If you are unhappy at work or if your job is not meeting your needs, look for another one. Pray and ask God to help you find a right job, but don't complain about the one you have while you search. Instead, when you go to work each day, thank God that you have a job. Even though you may not like your job, there are countless people in your city who would love to have it because they don't have one at all.

We cannot complain our way into a better position in life, and if we are going to complain about something, then we shouldn't bother praying about it.

CHAPTER 9

The Power of Thank You

At times our own light goes out and is rekindled by a spark from another person. Each of us has cause to think with deep gratitude of those who have lighted the flame within us.

Albert Schweitzer

The apostle Paul writes in 1 Thessalonians 5:11: "Therefore encourage (admonish, exhort) one another and edify (strengthen and build up) one another, just as you are doing" (AMPC).

The way to develop the best in people is through encouragement and appreciation. The way to get the worst from them is through continually bringing up their faults without mentioning the things they do well. Expressions of gratitude and encouragement build the spirit (the inner being) and strengthen people to try harder than ever to be better, but faultfinding breaks the spirit and causes them to feel hopeless and give up. This chapter includes several stories that I believe will help you see clearly how easy and necessary it is to express gratitude and encouragement to people.

Say Thank You for Thankless Jobs

When I ran across this story, I wanted to share it with you. I hope it will inspire you:

The janitorial industry is among the most thankless industries in North America. Ask yourself, when was the last time you thanked a janitor for doing a bang-up job? Don't blame yourself, part of a janitor's job is to be unnoticed like a stealthy ninja. We all love that our schools, shops, offices, and public spaces are clean and shiny, but seldom do we go out of our way to acknowledge those responsible for our sparkling surroundings.

When we saw this heartwarming post from a janitor, who met Keanu Reeves (and apparently, the celeb bought a store for him)...well...we just melted a little. This isn't a one-off either, on many occasions, Mr. Reeves has been known to commit extraordinary acts of kindness for complete strangers.

Randolph Gregory, a janitor living in St. Louis posted this very inspiring tale of legendary generosity, and it has been getting a lot of attention:

"I have been working as a janitor for the past 7 years, wiping the floor every day, and breaking my back to feed my family until I met Keanu Reeves 5 days ago at the restaurant where I work in St. Louis, and now I'm a shop owner thanks to him."[6]

Many people do thankless jobs that make life cleaner, safer, easier, or better in other ways for the people around them, including you and me. Let's make a point of thanking the people who clean our buildings and the bathrooms in the stores where we shop and anyone else whose job may not draw much appreciation. We may not be in a position to buy them a store or give an expensive gift, but saying thank you doesn't cost anything.

> *Saying thank you doesn't cost anything.*

My daughter once bought a thank-you card and a gift card to a restaurant and gave it to the garbage collector the next time he came to pick up her garbage. I am sure there are countless ways we could encourage people through simple words of appreciation if we would only think creatively.

I want to say it again: *Thank you* has power in it. It contains the power to encourage and to motivate a person to keep going, the power to lift them up and change what might have been a bad day into a good one.

The following story shows that getting no

appreciation can cause a person to quit and give up, while a thank you can give them the strength to keep going:

A lady worked as a janitor in a company for many years.

Now being a janitor is a pretty thankless job, which many of us might consider as a "dirty" job or at least pretty far down the totem pole. In other words, probably not a whole lot of fun.

It happened the company changed owners. Within a few days, the new owner wrote a personal thank-you card to every employee in the company. He had his assistant go around and hand them out.

When the lady received and opened her card, she burst into tears. She asked if she could be excused from work. Thinking she was sick, she was allowed to leave for the rest of the day.

What the story was—they found out a few days later—she had never received even a verbal thank you from the previous owners and management—much less a personal card.

And she had worked there 20 or 30 years!

So she was really touched when the new owner sent her a card of appreciation.

And...she had been thinking the change of ownership was probably a good time to quit.

And...she was planning to let them know *that very day*.

Which she didn't. Because the little time, the little extra effort of the owner to send a little business thank-you card, helped the lady change her mind.[7]

Be an Encourager

I will ask the Father, and He will give you another Helper (Comforter, Advocate, Intercessor—Counselor, Strengthener, Standby), to be with you forever—the Spirit of Truth...He (the Holy Spirit) remains with you continually and will be in you.

John 14:16–17 AMP

The original Greek text of John 14:16 refers to the Holy Spirit as Parakletos, which is Paraclete in English, and means the "Helper," or the

"One Who Walks Alongside Of." Perhaps the best English word we can use to describe this is the word *encourager*. If the Holy Spirit who lives in us is an encourager, then we should also be encouragers. He will show us ways to encourage one another if we will ask Him and follow His guidance. Just as my daughter had the idea to give her garbage collector a thank-you note with a gift card attached, the Holy Spirit will inspire us with creative ways to bless people if we will be sensitive and listen for His guidance.

Jesus did not "show favoritism" (Romans 2:11), meaning that He treated all people the same, regardless of their status or position in life. God's Word teaches us not to honor a rich man while dishonoring the downtrodden and poor person (James 2:3–4). The Bible also says that people who oppress the poor show "contempt for their Maker" (Proverbs 14:31). What does it mean to oppress another person? I think it means that we could help them but don't bother to do so, or that we treat them dishonorably, or perhaps ignore them altogether. We reveal more about our character through the way we treat people the world considers lowly than through the way we treat those considered wealthy or influential. Pride looks down on an individual it perceives as unimportant, but humility lowers itself in order to lift others up.

Exhort, Edify, and Encourage

How wonderful it is to give and receive encouragement, which means to give someone courage to keep pursuing their dreams and goals and not to give up during hard times. We all need that from time to time, and one of the best ways we can be assured of getting it when we need it is to always give it away. Jesus said we should treat others as we want to be treated (Matthew 7:12). If we all obeyed this one instruction, we would not have many of the problems we encounter in the world today.

In Romans 12:6–8 we find a list of the motivational gifts that God distributes as He desires to various people: prophesying, serving, teaching, encouraging, giving, leading, and showing mercy. Surely, encouragement is important since it is one of the gifts that God gives in order for His people to be strengthened and built up. I know people who have the gift of encouragement, and it is impossible to be around them and not leave their presence feeling better about yourself than when you arrived.

If encouragement is one of your strengths, please realize that it is such an important God-given ability. Everyone is instructed to encourage others, but those with a special gift of encouragement give it all the time to anyone and everyone they meet. It just flows out of them like a river. Jesus once said that rivers of living water would flow out from within us (John 7:38). Perhaps encouraging others is part of what He meant.

We live in a world that seems to enjoy tearing people down. Between social media, reality shows, talk radio, and conversations among people, we are not lacking in critical judgment, gossip, faultfinding, and believing and reporting the worst news possible. We should be building people up, not putting them down.

> We should be building people up, not putting them down.

Speaking words filled with death is the habit of the world, but it should not be so among God's people.

The church grows as we build up and edify others. Paul wrote to the Romans telling them to "make every effort to do what leads to peace and to mutual edification" (Romans 14:19). I rarely hear anyone use the word *edification*. In case you are not familiar with it, to *edify* is another way of saying "to encourage" or "to lift up."

Romans 14:19 teaches us that we must make an effort to edify and encourage. This may not always come naturally, but we can and should choose to do it regularly. When we edify someone, we instruct, improve, and uplift them. We can do this in many ways. We can use our words, our money, and our physical labor to offer encouragement and edification.

Yesterday Dave and I had an opportunity to use our money to encourage someone. I received a text message from a friend asking if we would join with several other couples to pay an elderly woman's property taxes. She has no family, and although she has enough to live a meager life throughout the year and her home is paid for, she cannot afford the year-end taxes. Of course, we said yes and sent the amount the Lord put on our heart. Can you imagine how encouraged this woman will be when she learns that her taxes have

> *If you live to give instead of to get, you will always have plenty and joy to go with it.*

been paid, mostly by people she doesn't even know? It cost some money, but if we live to give instead of to get, we will always have plenty and joy to go with it.

We regularly hear stories of those who volunteer their time and talent to help rebuild homes for people who have lost their in hurricanes, floods, fires, and other disasters. Yes, there are people who encourage, but there are more who don't than those who do. Galatians 6:10 urges us: "As we have opportunity, let us do good to all people, especially to those who belong to the family of believers."

Are you letting opportunities to encourage others pass you by? Do you hear of needs and ignore them because you don't want to sacrifice or make the effort to do anything about them? I'm sure we all feel this way at times, but let's ask God to regularly put opportunities to encourage others in our path, and when He does, let's follow through with action.

> Are you letting opportunities to encourage others pass you by?

Being an encouraging person really isn't difficult. You can encourage someone by simply telling them that the color they are wearing looks good on them or that you like their shoes. "I appreciate you" and "I'm glad you are in my life" are simple phrases that make a big impact.

I have a few people in my life who regularly encourage me, and I appreciate them greatly. I recently purchased a gift for one of them and told her how much I appreciate her encouragement and prayers. When people do encourage you, thank them. And when others thank you for encouraging them, don't answer with something like "Oh, it was nothing" or "No problem," because when you do, it feels rather flat to the one who makes the effort to thank you. A simple "I appreciate that" is all that is needed. I love what my administrative assistant says when she does something for me and I thank her. She replies, "My pleasure!"

Lifting Someone's Load

Life is often difficult for some people, and they are hungry for encouragement. We can lift their burden or lighten their load with a few simple, heartfelt words. One way to encourage people when they are hurting is to simply call or text to check on them. Just tell them you are thinking of them and wanted to check and see how they are doing.

When we are going through a difficult time in life, we can also encourage others, and it will help us feel better. I recently read this short story by Marc Chernoff.

> This past holiday season Angel [my wife] and I stayed at a hotel near her parents' house in South Florida. On Christmas Eve we met a family of six who were staying at the same hotel. We saw them relaxing in the lobby by the Christmas tree, sharing stories and laughing. So on our way out, Angel and I wished them a happy holiday season and asked where they were from. "Oh, we're from here," the mother said. "Our house burned down to the ground yesterday, but miraculously, all of us made it out safely. And that makes this a very merry Christmas." Her words and her family's optimistic attitude made me smile. They reminded me that the most fulfilling moments in life come when we finally find the courage to let go of what we can't change.[8]

The family who lost their home in a fire had such a good attitude that they ended up encouraging the couple on vacation.

Remember Those Who Have Helped You

As we travel through life, we meet many people. Some of them hurt and disappoint us, but many of them help us and leave a lasting impact for good. As a matter of fact, we might not be where we are today had God not placed them in our lives.

I can think of several people who have impacted my life in significant, positive ways. How about you? People who gave me some of my first opportunities to teach God's Word. People who worked without pay when our ministry first began and we had no money for salaries. The men who volunteered their time after working all day to finish our basement and turn it into office space. People who believed in God's call on my life and encouraged me when things were difficult and I felt I couldn't go on. One particular woman has prayed for me daily for more than thirty years. And a whole host of others. I think of those people often, and I still thank God for them. I also send Christmas gifts yearly and let people know how important they were and still are to me.

Teacher Appreciation

I heard a story about a group of men who were talking about people who had influenced their lives and for whom they were grateful. One man remembered a high school teacher who had introduced him to the poetry of Alfred, Lord Tennyson. He decided to write and thank her. In time, written in a feeble scrawl, came the teacher's reply:

> My Dear Willie: I can't tell you how much your note meant to me. I am in my eighties, living alone in a small room, cooking my own meals, lonely, like the last autumn leaf lingering behind. You will be interested to know that I taught school for fifty years, and yours is the first note of appreciation I have ever received. It came on a blue, cold morning, and it cheered me as nothing has for years.

This story shows the power of thank you and reminds us of how quickly we forget those who have helped us along our way through life. Let's all remember this story and ask God to remind us of people we can remember and encourage, perhaps with a note or a phone call. Reaching out to them will only take a tiny bit of effort for us, but it may mean the world to them, as it did to Willie's teacher.

Practice the Power

As you can see, there is an interesting relationship between encouragement and appreciation. When we encourage someone, they often feel appreciated, and when we thank them for something, they feel encouraged. There are many practical ways to encourage people or thank them for what they do in the everyday, ordinary aspects of life. Here are twelve specific gestures of encouragement or appreciation you might consider. I challenge you to use your creativity and find other ways to bless the people around you:

- Thank the people who deliver mail or packages to your home safely.
- Encourage a single mother by telling her she is special and giving her a gift card for

a manicure or a manicure-pedicure combination. Then offer to babysit while she has it done.

- Thank the person who checks out your shopping at the grocery store.
- Thank the driver of the bus, taxi, or other vehicle for getting you to your destination safely.
- Ask an elderly neighbor if you can run any errands or take care of any household chores for them. Even changing a light bulb or an air filter could be helpful and encouraging to someone.
- Buy a meal for a member of the armed services or someone else who keeps your neighborhood or country safe and say, "I just wanted you to know I appreciate what you do for us."
- Offer cold water to the people who take care of your lawn during hot weather, and thank them for making it look nice.
- When you see a neighbor trimming hedges, washing their car, or working on their house, simply wave and say, "Looks good!"
- When you have received good service in a restaurant, in addition to recognizing it

with a nice tip, consider also saying, "We really appreciate the good service you've given us today."

- When you notice something positive about someone, such as a new hairstyle or a nice-looking outfit, don't just think *That looks nice*; go ahead and verbalize a compliment.
- When someone allows you to go in front of them in traffic, offer a quick wave as a way of saying thank you.
- When someone helps you at the doctor's office or the dentist's office, say thank you. Many people don't like going to medical or dental visits, so they are not always glad to see the people who help them. Even if you have to get a shot or have a cavity filled, and it's not fun or pleasant, you can still appreciate the skill of the people who help you. They help you stay healthy, and we can all be grateful for our health.

CHAPTER 10

Thank You! Thank You! Thank You!

Bring me a worm that can comprehend a man, and then I will show you a man that can comprehend the Triune God.

John Wesley

No person can understand the Trinity (Triune God; Father, Son, and Holy Spirit) with their mind; the Trinity can only be understood and believed in with the heart. Although the Bible never uses the word *Trinity*, there are ample scriptures that mention God the Father, Jesus the Son, and the Holy Spirit. We serve one God who manifests in three persons, each playing a vital role in our lives.

I will not attempt a long theological teaching on the Trinity in this book, but I do want to remind you how important it is for us to be thankful for God the Father, Jesus, and the Holy Spirit, and to remind ourselves frequently of the role each one plays in our life. Here are several scriptures that clearly show all three persons of the Trinity working together as one.

But the Advocate, the Holy Spirit, whom the Father will send in my name, will teach you all things and will remind you of everything I have said to you.

John 14:26

Therefore go and make disciples of all nations, baptizing them in the name of the Father and of the Son and of the Holy Spirit.

Matthew 28:19

The Holy Spirit descended on him in bodily form like a dove. And a voice came from heaven: "You are my Son, whom I love; with you I am well pleased."

Luke 3:22

God anointed Jesus of Nazareth with the Holy Spirit and power, and...he went around doing good and healing all who were under the power of the devil, because God was with him.

Acts 10:38

May the grace of the Lord Jesus Christ, and the love of God, and the fellowship of the Holy Spirit be with you all.

2 Corinthians 13:14

Thanking Father God

Ephesians 5:20 specifically mentions thanking God the Father, encouraging readers to be "always giving thanks to God the Father for everything, in the name of our Lord Jesus Christ." In addition to offering thanks to Father God, we also have the great privilege of praying and asking Him for anything we want or need, but we ask in Jesus' name. God's Word teaches us to pray to the Father, in Jesus' name, and in the power of the Holy Spirit (Matthew 6:6; John 14:13–14; Ephesians 6:18). So, we see that the Trinity is involved in all of our prayers, as well as in other aspects of our spiritual life.

In my morning prayers, I often thank God for Himself. I thank Him also for all that He has done, is doing, and will do for me. But I like to thank Him simply for Himself. If He never did anything for any of us, the simple fact that He loves us would still be a great blessing and privilege. I can't imagine how awful life would be without God. I am thankful for my relationship with Him, which is always growing.

In my early years as a Christian, I focused on what I needed God to do for me, and I was thankful for those things when He provided them. But at that time, I wasn't spiritually mature enough to realize that I needed to seek His face (presence) and not merely His hand (what He could give me). Most of us probably begin our relationship with God that way, but hopefully we grow beyond it.

I have four grown children and twelve grand-children, eight of whom are adults. I don't want them to call me or come to see me only when they want something. I want them to love me for who I am more than they love me for what I do for them. Interestingly enough, the more they love me for me, the more I want to do for them. Surely, if we are that way, then God is, too. We should always seek God, because He is wonder-ful, good, kind, loving, merciful, and just plain awesome. We need to count everything He does for us as a fringe benefit of our relationship with Him. The personal relationship we have with Him is more important than anything else.

I have developed the habit of always thank-ing God for Himself and for His presence in my life before I thank Him for all He does for me. Father God does and has done more for each of us than we could ever fully recognize.

Consider this list, which is certainly not complete, but does give you a good idea of who He is and ways He shows His love for us:

> *Always thank God for Himself and for His presence in your life.*

- God our Father is our provider (Philippians 4:19).
- He is always just, and He is righteous (right); He is holy, and He is love (Psalm 145:17; Leviticus 19:2; 1 John 4:8).
- He is sovereign, has all power, knows all things, and is everywhere at all times (1 Chronicles 29:11; Jeremiah 32:27; Romans 11:33; Proverbs 15:3).
- He created all that we see out of nothing, and all things are possible with Him (Hebrews 11:1–3; Matthew 19:26).
- He created us in our mother's womb with His own hand (Psalm 139:13).
- He hears and answers our prayers in His own way and timing (2 Chronicles 7:14; Psalm 27:13–14; Matthew 7:7).
- His thoughts toward us are more than the grains of the sand on the seashore (Psalm 139:17–18).

- His love for us is unconditional and never-ending. It is a perfect love that casts out fear (Jeremiah 31:3; 1 John 4:18).
- He sent and sacrificed His only Son to save us from our sins and open the way for us to have intimate fellowship with Him (John 3:16–17; 1 John 4:9–10).

Let us thank God daily for who He is and that He is in our lives, inviting us into close, intimate relationship with Him through our faith in Jesus Christ. What a privilege it is to get to know Him intimately and realize that He cares about us and about every aspect of our lives. We can never thank Him too much or too often.

Thanking Jesus

Jesus is God's Son, whom God sent to earth to save us from our sins. Sin separates us from God. But because of His death on the cross, our sins are forgiven, and we are free to enjoy a personal, unhindered, right relationship with God the Father.

We cannot even begin to fathom the sacrifice Jesus made for us and how much He suffered in our place when He came to earth and became a man so He might identify with us. He was fully man, yet fully God (Philippians 2:6–8; Hebrews 1:1–3; Colossians 2:9). He is called the Son of God and the Son of Man (John 10:36; Matthew 9:6). He can understand and identify with everything we suffer and experience, including our temptations, yet He never sinned—He was the perfect sacrifice (Hebrews 4:14–16). He was the spotless Lamb of God who sacrificed His life for us and took away our sins (John 1:29). His sacrifice was complete, and it was made once and for all (Hebrews 9:28; 10:12–14).

Under the Old Covenant (during Old Testament times, prior to Christ's birth, life, death, and resurrection), the people had to sacrifice animals over and over every year to have their sins temporarily *covered* (Hebrews 10:1–4). But under the New Covenant, Jesus shed His blood on the cross that our sins might be *washed away and atoned for* "once for all" (Hebrews 9:26; Romans 3:25). Because of Jesus' sacrifice, our sins can now be removed from us as far as the east is from the west (Psalm 103:12). We should always thank

> *Always thank Jesus for His precious blood, with which we have been made God's own.*

Jesus for His precious blood, with which we have been purchased and made God's own.

If we admit our sins and repent of them, God not only forgives them—He does not even remember them (Hebrews 8:12). The following eighteen verses from Hebrews 10 explain the freedom from sin we now have through Jesus Christ under the New Covenant. I believe that taking time to read these verses slowly, asking God to help you fully understand it, will be valuable for you.

Christ's Sacrifice Once for All

The law is only a shadow of the good things that are coming—not the realities themselves. For this reason it can never, by the same sacrifices repeated endlessly year after year, make perfect those who draw near to worship. Otherwise, would they not have stopped being offered? For the worshipers would have been cleansed once for all, and would no longer have felt guilty for their sins. But those sacrifices are an annual reminder of sins. It is impossible for the blood of bulls and goats to take away sins.

Therefore, when Christ came into the world, he said:

"Sacrifice and offering you did not desire,
but a body you prepared for me;
with burnt offerings and sin offerings
you were not pleased.
Then I said, 'Here I am—it is written
about me in the scroll—
I have come to do your will, my God.'"

First he said, "Sacrifices and offerings, burnt offerings and sin offerings you did not desire, nor were you pleased with them"— though they were offered in accordance with the law. Then he said, "Here I am, I have come to do your will." He sets aside the first to establish the second. And by that will, we have been made holy through the sacrifice of the body of Jesus Christ once for all.

Day after day every priest stands and performs his religious duties; again and again he offers the same sacrifices, which can never take away sins. But when this priest had offered for all time one sacrifice for sins, he sat down at the right hand of God, and since that time he waits for his enemies to be made his footstool. For by one sacrifice he has made perfect forever those who are being made holy.

The Holy Spirit also testifies to us about this. First he says:

"This is the covenant I will make with them

after that time, says the Lord.

I will put my laws in their hearts,

and I will write them on their minds."

Then he adds:

"Their sins and lawless acts

I will remember no more."

And where these have been forgiven, sacrifice for sin is no longer necessary.

Hebrews 10:1–18

The more our hearts grasp who Jesus is and what He has done for us, the more we will want to say thank You!

We Have Been Set Free

We have been set free from the tyranny of sin and guilt and from the fear of being rejected by God. Even though He does not approve of everything

we do, He never stops loving us and working with
us to help us change and
grow. Through His grace,
"He made us accepted"
in Jesus Christ (Ephesians
1:6 NKJV). Think about it:
You are loved and accepted
by God through your faith in Jesus Christ. This
is a reason to rejoice and to give thanks!

> *We have been
> set free from the
> tyranny of sin and
> guilt and from
> the fear of being
> rejected by God.*

Because of Jesus we can come boldly to
God's throne of grace without any fear of being
rejected:

> Let us then fearlessly and confidently and
> boldly draw near to the throne of grace
> (the throne of God's unmerited favor to
> us sinners), that we may receive mercy
> [for our failures] and find grace to help in
> good time for every need [appropriate help
> and well-timed help, coming just when we
> need it].
>
> Hebrews 4:16 AMPC

What has Jesus done for us? Think about these
truths:

- Jesus took the punishment that we deserved as sinners. He paid for (atoned for) our sins and set us free from the guilt connected to them. (Isaiah 53:4–5; 1 Peter 2:24).
- He defeated Satan for us (1 John 3:8; Galatians 1:4; Colossians 2:15).
- Although Satan may come against us, we are already more than conquerors through Jesus, who loves us (Romans 8:37).
- Jesus justifies us and makes us able to stand before God, clothed in His own righteousness (Romans 5:1; 2 Corinthians 5:21).
- He restored our broken relationship with God (2 Corinthians 5:18).
- Jesus is the name above every other name (Philippians 2:9–11), and He has given us the privilege of praying in His name. When we do so, we present to God all that Jesus is, not what we are: "My Father will grant you whatever you ask in My Name [as presenting all that I AM]" (John 16:23 AMPC).
- Through Jesus, we are born again by placing our faith in Him. Old things pass away and all things become new (2 Corinthians 5:17).

I could go on and on, but I am sure you can see that we have ample reason to thank Jesus continually for what He has done and continues to do for us.

When He ascended on high to take His seat at the right hand of God, He did not leave us alone, but He sent the Holy Spirit to live with and in us (John 14:16–17; 20:22). When Jesus was dying on the cross and paying for our sins, He said, "It is finished" (John 19:30). He meant that the old system of rules, regulations, and insufficient sacrifices for sin was—and is—finished. Jesus did everything that needed to be done, and our part is to believe that what He says in His Word is true and live by it.

Thanking the Holy Spirit

I believe, and many people agree, that the Holy Spirit does not receive the attention due Him. Although Jesus purchased our freedom from sin, our right standing with God, our justification, and our sanctification (holiness), the Holy Spirit is the one who works these benefits into our daily life and behavior. When Jesus ascended to the right hand of the throne of God, He sent the

Holy Spirit to represent Him on earth and to continue His work through us (John 7:38–39; Acts 1:8; 2:32–33). He told His disciples that they would be better off when He left the earth because then He would send the Holy Spirit (John 16:7).

How could anyone be better off without Jesus' physical presence? Jesus lived on earth in the form of a man, and therefore He could only be one place at a time. But the Holy Spirit can be everywhere all the time because He is not confined to one body. He lives in all of us who believe in Jesus and have received Him as our Lord and Savior. He can work in and through each of us at the same time and in many different places. Jesus said that we would not only do the works He did, but that we would do greater things (John 14:12). I believe this is accomplished through the Holy Spirit.

God sent the Holy Spirit to earth for the purpose of teaching us all the truth expressed in God's Word (John 16:13). He works out the process of sanctification in our lives as we cooperate with Him, being obedient to His guidance (2 Thessalonians 2:13).

The Holy Spirit is a wonderful friend who

reveals Jesus to us and in us (John 15:26). He is with us at all times and lives in us (John 14:17). Because He is in us, His fruit is in us, and He works with us to develop that fruit until it is in full bloom in our lives and can be seen as a witness to the world of how God changes a person who submits to Him. The fruit of the Holy Spirit is "love, joy, peace, forbear-

> The Holy Spirit is a wonderful friend who reveals Jesus to us and in us.

ance, kindness, goodness, faithfulness, gentleness and self-control" (Galatians 5:22–23).

The Holy Spirit is with us always to represent Jesus and to help us in everything. He is our Advocate and our Intercessor. He teaches us, guides us, helps us, and convicts us of sin, which is amazingly beneficial (John 15:26; 16:7–15; Romans 8:26–27). When we receive His conviction (not condemnation), He shows us what we are doing that does not please God. If we admit it and repent, then He helps us overcome it.

As a means of understanding the fruit of the Holy Spirit, think of a muscle. We all have muscles, but unless they are developed through use they will not be seen and will be of little value to us. The fruit of the Spirit is the same way. We have it in us, but it is developed and made strong through use. Patience, for example, can only be developed through trial, according to *Vine's Expository Dictionary*. In other words, we must be in a position to need to use patience in order for it to grow and become strong. This principle of growth through use is true for all nine of the fruit of the Spirit.

When a Christian has this fruit in his or her life, it draws people to Jesus. Therefore, we should seek with all zeal a relationship with the Holy Spirit and the fruit that this relationship produces. It is the work of the Holy Spirit to develop this fruit and holiness in the believer. Consider these additional ways the Holy Spirit works for us and in us:

- The Holy Spirit convicts us of sin and convinces us of righteousness (John 16:8).
- He leads and guides us (Romans 8:14; Acts 8:29).
- He helps us pray when we do not know how to pray as we should (Romans 8:26–27).
- He anoints us with power and ability to do what God has called us to do (Acts 1:8).
- He always glorifies Jesus and the Father,

just as Jesus always glorifies the Father (John 16:14).

- He is always standing by to help us in any way that we need help (Romans 8:1–2; Acts 2:38–39; Ephesians 3:16–20).
- He knows the deep things of God and shows us what God has freely given us (1 Corinthians 2:9–12).
- He distributes spiritual gifts (1 Corinthians 12:11).

There is no competition within the Trinity; each is for the other and they work together for one purpose—for the will of God to be done in the earth through believers (Matthew 28:19). Jesus prayed for us that we would be one even as He and the Father are one (John 17:11, 21–22). I think it is safe to say that we still have work to do to accomplish this kind of unity, but I believe each of us should do our part in moving toward that goal.

My Eyes Were Opened

I went to church for many years, and though I heard the Holy Spirit mentioned in baptisms and benedictions, I was clueless about His role in my daily life. Because of that, I also lacked the strength He gives. I was a powerless, miserable Christian who had no victory, peace, or true joy. I was born again, I loved the Lord, and I totally believe I would have gone to heaven had I died, but I lived a defeated life and had no ability to be a witness to anyone else who needed Jesus. I served on the evangelism team of our church, and each week, I went door-to-door inviting people to come to church,

> I could "do" witnessing, but I was not a witness.

but I was not a witness for God in my daily life or behavior. I could "do" witnessing, but I was not a witness.

I cried out to God for change in my life, and thankfully He touched me powerfully, introducing me to the Holy Spirit in a whole new way, which transformed me and changed the direction of my life. This took place in 1976, and a few months later, God gave me an intense desire to teach His Word. He spoke to my heart in a way I could not deny. Following that call has been my passion ever since.

It is the Holy Spirit who changes us by the grace of God as we submit our lives to Him to work in us. We should thank Him frequently for His patience with us, as well as for the progress we make in spiritual maturity.

> *It is the Holy Spirit who changes us by the grace of God as we submit our lives to Him to work in us.*

It is the Holy Spirit who empowers us for service in God's Kingdom. He imparts gifts to each of us as He sees fit (1 Corinthians 12:1, 4–11). As we exercise those gifts, each one of us doing our part, the kingdom of God grows, and souls are snatched from the gates of hell (meaning that people receive Jesus as their Savior).

The Holy Spirit's work in the earthly realm and in each of us is so amazing that all I can say is "Thank You, Father, for the Holy Spirit. Thank You, Jesus, for sending Him, and thank You, Holy Spirit, for coming to earth to help us make our journey through this life on earth to our home in heaven. I am grateful that we are never alone, and I thank You for always being with us, guiding us on the right path, and strengthening us to do God's will."

It is important to thank God, thank Jesus, and thank the Holy Spirit for all that they continually do for us. When we speak to God, we are speaking to all three persons of the Trinity, yet I feel it is important for us to be aware of the diversity of their roles in our lives and to be thankful for each of them.

CHAPTER 11

Humility and Gratitude

I will forever remain humble because I know I could have less. I will always be grateful because I know I've had less.

Author Unknown

Thankfulness is the overflow of a humble heart, just as complaining is the overflow of a proud heart. Proud people think they deserve everything they have and even think they should have more. But humble people realize they deserve nothing and are therefore extremely thankful for all that God has done for them.

My mother once said to me, "You should take good care of me. After all, I am your mother." I did take good care of her, because I felt it was my duty before God to do so, but when she made that statement, she had apparently forgotten that she knew about the sexual abuse I suffered at the hand of my father and did nothing to rescue me. Because of fear, she abandoned me to the situation and never even spoke to me about it until thirty years after I left home. She felt she was entitled to things she had done nothing to deserve.

Of course, God gives us many blessings we do not deserve. This is why He expects us to help even those who have hurt and abused us. I helped my parents not because I thought they deserved my help, but because I knew helping them was the right thing to do. It was what Jesus would have done. Helping them would have been a bit easier had they said, "We know we don't deserve it, but we really appreciate your help." However, they didn't say that, and I had to remember how often God has helped me when I didn't realize I didn't deserve it, either. Don't ever think that in God's eyes you are excused from helping people just because they don't deserve it.

Proud people think they are entitled to things they have not worked for. They are jealous of other people's blessings and even resent them for being blessed. I often say, "Don't be jealous of what someone else has if you don't want to do what they did to get it."

Complaining is the fruit of a proud heart. When we complain, it means that we think we deserve better than our circumstances have given us. God is happy to help us in any difficulty, but His Word states that if we humble ourselves "under God's mighty hand," He will "lift" us "up in due time" (1 Peter 5:6). The humble get the help, not the proud.

> Don't be jealous of what someone else has if you don't want to do what they did to get it.

Be Humble in Tough Times

Paul wrote to the Corinthians about the trials and troubles he and the group of believers who worked with him had experienced, noting that the difficulties were so severe they felt they had "despaired of life" and "received the sentence of death" (2 Corinthians 1:8–9). Then he explained the reason for this turn of events: "But this happened that we might not rely on ourselves but on God" (2 Corinthians 1:9). It was necessary for Paul and those ministering with him always to remain humble and reliant on God, and apparently God let them practice occasionally so they didn't forget it.

We see a similar example later in 2 Corinthians, when Paul wrote of the need to be humble in the face of "surpassingly great revelations" (12:7) God had given him:

> Therefore, in order to keep me from becoming conceited, I was given a thorn in my flesh, a messenger of Satan, to torment me. Three times I pleaded with the Lord to take it away from me. But he said to me, "My grace is sufficient for you, for my power

is made perfect in weakness." Therefore I will boast all the more gladly about my weaknesses, so that Christ's power may rest on me.

2 Corinthians 12:7–9

Difficulty Turns to Gratitude

Those of us who have endured times of need in our lives and have had to do with less are usually very thankful when we experience increase. I know I am. I recall needing to shop at garage sales for six years and being excited and thankful when I found a pair of new tennis shoes for one of my children for two dollars. I am certain that I complained during those years, but now I am thankful for them because remembering them makes me appreciate and be thankful for everything God has blessed me with now.

I also remember the early days of our ministry, when we traveled to speaking engagements in an old van with bald tires and rusty wheel wells, which we purchased for sixteen hundred dollars. In those days, we couldn't afford to stay in hotels after speaking engagements, so we headed home. When Dave became too tired to drive, we parked in parking lots of fast-food restaurants so he could sleep for a while.

In addition, I have memories of visiting my grandparents in southeastern Missouri and having no indoor plumbing. The outhouses (as the small, dark, shack-like buildings that housed outdoor toilets were called) were very cold or very hot, depending on the weather, and if they were hot, the stink was terrible. There was no toilet tissue, so we used old Sears catalogs or newspaper. There were plenty of spiders and other bugs that made the experience even more distasteful. Let's just say that I didn't go to the toilet unless I *really* needed to use it.

When we needed water, we had to go to the pump to get it. When we wanted to iron clothes, we had no electric irons. The house had no electricity anyway, so we had to heat heavy irons made of cast iron on a stove and then try to iron the piece of clothing before the iron cooled off. The material wasn't permanent press but a heavy cotton that wasn't easy to iron.

There was no heat in the house at night because the wood stove would go out. Everyone would wait for Grandpa to get up in the morning and get the fire going before we got out of bed, and when we did, we ran to the room where the stove was. I don't remember complaining, because that was just the way life was back then. I think we complained less during those times than we do now.

I've also been to places in India where the toilets are simply holes in the floor. For some reason, I have never been able to master using them, no matter how bad I have to go. I don't know if you are thankful for your toilet, but I am thankful for mine!

I am so thankful now for my home. I am also very thankful that when we hold conferences or do speaking engagements we can actually fly to other cities and stay in hotels. Occasionally, I find myself complaining about a hotel room, but humility would have me remember when there was no money for hotel rooms at all and remind me to be thankful for what I have.

Sometimes we are thankful out of the overflow of our hearts, and sometimes we have to remind ourselves to be thankful by looking back at how life used to be compared to how it is now. We don't want to let what was once a blessing to us become

> *Don't let what was once a blessing become an expectation and a right.*

an expectation and a right. Let's always thank God for His goodness and remember with grateful hearts all He has done for us.

You Owe Me

Have you ever heard the statement that someone has a chip on their shoulder? This means they are angry because they feel they have been mistreated and think the people who hurt them now owe them something. I know this feeling because I had a chip on my shoulder after suffering from sexual abuse from my father. I had a bitter, self-pitying attitude and always felt that people should treat me better than they did. Of course, the way I was treated growing up was wrong, but I shouldn't have expected everyone around me to try to compensate me for it.

My problem was that I was trying to collect from people who had nothing to do with my pain. I was set free when I read in Matthew 18:23–35 about a man who owed a debt, but "because he could not pay" (v. 25 AMPC), the person to whom he was indebted forgave him. The words *he could not pay* seemed to jump out at me, and at that moment, I realized that my father could never pay me back. He took my innocence, my childhood, my self-respect, and my confidence. How could he give those qualities back to me? I also realized that no human being could pay me back, but that God would somehow restore all I had lost if I would turn my brokenness over to Him and follow His guidelines for healing. He promised to be my recompense, and I could count on Him to give me a double blessing for my former trouble (Isaiah 61:7). In other words, I could expect His blessings to far outweigh the pain and hardships I had endured.

I realized I could forgive all the people who hurt me, let go of the past, and take responsibility for my future. When I stopped trying to collect from the people who could never pay me anything and allowed God to take over, He began healing me and blessing my life in ways that no one else could.

It is said that our current generation is an entitled generation—a "me, me, me" generation that expects to be given what in reality they should work to earn. God created us to work and earn things by being responsible and using wisdom, and He promises that we will experience

increase as we do. He
put Adam and Eve in
the Garden of Eden,
and it contained every-
thing they needed, but
they were told to "work

> *God created us to
> work and earn things
> by being responsible
> and using wisdom.*

it and take care of it" (Genesis 2:15).

Vocabulary.com says, "The adjective *entitled*
means that you have a legal right to something.
If you are *entitled* to your mother's house when
she passes away, that means it's written in her will
that she gave it to you." Sometimes, though, people
feel they are entitled to special treatment because
they think they are more worthy than others.

God's Word warns us not to think more
highly of ourselves than we ought to but to realize that everything we have and everything we
can do is because of God's grace (Romans 12:3).

If a person is especially talented or intelligent,
their abilities are gifts from God and not qualities that should make them think they are better
than anyone else. Realizing that our abilities are
God-given keeps us thankful for them, rather
than causing us to be excessively proud. Pride
always ends up causing problems.

Proverbs 6:16–19 lists things the Lord hates,

and first on the list is "haughty eyes" (v. 17). This means pride. The Lord hates pride because He knows that it eventually leads to trouble for us.

Proverbs also states that pride always comes before a fall or before destruction (Proverbs 16:18). A thankful heart opens the door for blessings from God, but a proud one blocks them. To be thankful, we must first be humble.

> To be thankful, we must first be humble.

Webster's 1828 dictionary defines *pride* as "inordinate self-esteem; an unreasonable conceit of one's own superiority in talents, beauty, wealth, accomplishments, rank or elevation in office, which manifests itself in lofty airs, distance, reserve, and often in contempt of others."

The definition of *humility* is "In ethics, freedom from pride and arrogance; humbleness of mind; a modest estimate of one's own worth. In theology, humility consists in lowliness of mind; a deep sense of one's own unworthiness in the sight of God, self-abasement, penitence for sin, and submission to the divine will."

Our worth and value are found in Christ, not in our own abilities, and we should always remember this.

Humility Must Be Sought and Practiced

Andrew Murray, a great author and revivalist said, "Humility is not a thing that will come of itself, but it must be made the object of special desire and prayer and faith." I highly recommend his book simply titled *Humility*.[9] I remember the profound effect it had on me the first time I read it. It is one of my favorite books, and I have read it and reread it several times. Reading this short volume was my first encounter with the importance of humility—one that I desperately needed, even though I was not aware of that need.

Consider these statements that Andrew Murray made about humility, which remind us of its infinite value.

- "The deepest humility is the secret of the truest happiness, of a joy that nothing can destroy" (p. 71).
- "Humility...is the displacement of self by the enthronement of God" (p. 47).
- "Unless pride dies in you, nothing of heaven can live in you" (p. 5).

- "Men sometimes speak as if humility and meekness would rob us of that which is noble and bold and manlike. Oh, that all would believe that this is the nobility of the kingdom of heaven, that this is the royal spirit that the King of heaven displayed, that this is Godlike, to humble oneself, to become the servant of all!" (p. 26).
- "Humility is simply the disposition which prepares the soul for living on trust" (p. 54).
- "Our humility before God has no value, except as it prepares us to reveal the humility of Jesus to our fellow men" (p. 35).
- "Here is the path to the higher life. Down, lower down!...Just as water ever seeks and fills the lowest place, so the moment God finds the creature [people] abased and empty, His glory and power flow in to exalt and to bless" (p. 25).
- "His humility is our salvation. His salvation is our humility" (p. 3).
- "Humility, the place of entire dependence upon God, is, from the very nature of things, the first duty and the highest virtue of the creature. And so pride, or the loss of humility, is the root of every sin and evil" (p. 2).

Another resource I would like to recommend can be found on the internet and downloaded free. It is called the "Fifty Fruits of Pride."[10] If you ever have a day when you find yourself feeling entitled or better than others, just read over this list and you will soon find humility returning.

If we truly believe we deserve nothing and are entitled to nothing, I wonder how many things we previously felt we had a right to would become things we are now thankful for. God wants us to be very blessed. He says that everything we lay our hand to will prosper and succeed, but this promise is attached to an instruction to give generously to the poor:

> Give generously to them and do so without a grudging heart; then because of this the Lord your God will bless you in all your work and in everything you put your hand to. There will always be poor people in the land. Therefore I command you to be openhanded toward your fellow Israelites who are poor and needy in your land.
>
> Deuteronomy 15:10–11

We cannot be thankful without humility,

> *Generosity is proof of a humble and thankful heart.*

and only through humility and gratitude will we find the desire to give generously to help those less fortunate than we are. I might even go so far as to say that generosity is proof of a humble and thankful heart.

CHAPTER 12

Gratitude Is a Weapon

For the weapons of our warfare are not carnal but mighty in God for pulling down strongholds.

2 Corinthians 10:4 NKJV

God's Word teaches us that we are in a spiritual war and that He has given us weapons to help us win this conflict. We have an enemy, and the Bible refers to him as Satan or the devil. Many people shy away from talk about the devil, but in my opinion, that is foolish. Jesus dealt with the devil. He spoke to him (Luke 4:1–13), He resisted him, and He tells us to do the same (Matthew 16:23; James 4:7). We won't resist an enemy if we don't believe he exists. Instead, we will blame our troubles on God or on other people, when in reality Satan is behind them.

The devil's goal is either to keep us out of a relationship with God through Jesus or to prevent us from knowing and claiming for ourselves our inheritance in Christ. Our misery is the devil's greatest joy. His purpose is to steal,

> *Our misery is the devil's greatest joy.*

kill, and destroy (John 10:10). We must understand that the devil works not only independently through direct attack, but also through unwitting people who unknowingly become his vessels. In Matthew 16, we see him using Peter to try to cause Jesus to stumble. Jesus recognized what was taking place, looked directly at Peter, and said, "Get behind me, Satan!" (Matthew 16:23). He wasn't saying that Peter *was* Satan, but that Satan was working *through* Peter.

When God called me to teach His Word, I experienced a lot of opposition from friends and family who thought I was making a mistake. Although they meant well, they were wrong, and I am grateful that I had the grace to go with God instead of being a people-pleaser. Paul said that when a "wide door of opportunity" opened to him, with it came "many adversaries" (1 Corinthians 16:9 AMPC). We should remember that Satan always opposes anything good and anything that brings progress.

We are in a war between good and evil, and Romans 12:21 tells us that we overcome evil with good. The devil will try with all his might to keep us from being or doing good and will tempt us to do evil. But we can defeat him through recognizing his lies and deception, continuing to follow God, and doing what is right. Being thankful at all times in all situations is the right thing to do and will help us win our battles.

See and Speak the Good

Did you know that being negative can be the same as what some Bible translations call bringing "an evil report" (Numbers 13:32 AMPC; KJV)? When Moses sent twelve men to spy out the land of Canaan, ten returned with a negative report, rehearsing everything they found wrong in the land, while only two came back with a positive report (Numbers 13:26–33).

We don't need to ignore negative situations, but we can certainly avoid being totally negative by also seeing and speaking about the good. The ten negative spies might have said, "There are giants in the land that are much larger than we are. But God is on our side, and the fruit there is very large and abundant," but they ignored the good and their report focused on the problems. From Numbers 13:32, we can see that focusing on and talking about the negatives in life is evil.

Joshua and Caleb were the two men who brought back a good report. They were men of faith and saw the positive aspects of the land. They were the ones allowed to enter into the land and to lead into it those who had been born in the wilderness during the Israelites' travels.

The two who were positive were winners, and the ten who were negative were losers, and the devil stole their inheritance.

In 2 Chronicles 20, we see an account of Jehoshaphat being attacked by his enemies. As he sought God for direction, God directed him to take his position and wait on Him. God also told him that he would not need to fight in the battle. Jehoshaphat did as God directed and sent singers out ahead of his army, singing, *"Give thanks to the Lord, for his love endures forever"* (2 Chronicles 20:21, emphasis mine). They continued to sing and worship, and Jehoshaphat continued to pray, and something amazing took place: Their enemies became so confused that they slaughtered one another. Just as God had promised, they didn't need to fight that battle. When the Israelites went into the enemy's camp, they found all the men dead, and they carried off their equipment, clothing, and other valuables. The plunder was so great that they needed three days to carry it all away (2 Chronicles 20:20–25). When the devil does something to make us miserable and we continue thanking God, it does confuse him.

Jehoshaphat's story is a faith-building story.

God's people won a major victory through giving thanks, worshipping, and praying. I wonder how often we lose our battles because we try to make things happen in our own strength when more gratitude and worship is what we really need.

When we give thanks, we shift our focus away from our problems and onto the answers. This is a powerful weapon of spiritual warfare.

> *Giving thanks shifts your focus away from your problems and onto the answers.*

Thanksgiving and God's Presence

Thanksgiving ushers in the presence of God, and when God is present, we always have victory. In 2 Chronicles 5, we read that the ark of God was brought into the temple, and verses 13–14 show us a powerful picture of what God's presence and glory looked like:

> The trumpeters and musicians joined in unison to give praise and thanks to the Lord. Accompanied by trumpets, cymbals and other instruments, the singers raised

their voices in praise to the Lord and sang: "He is good; his love endures forever." Then the temple of the Lord was filled with the cloud, and the priests could not perform their service because of the cloud, for the glory of the Lord filled the temple of God.

The cloud mentioned in this passage was the cloud of God's presence, the same cloud that followed the Israelites by day through the wilderness (Exodus 13:21–22).

When we remain thankful, we remain in faith, but complaining cultivates doubt and creates an atmosphere for worry and anxiety. When these emotions are present, our problems remain, but thanksgiving releases faith, hope, and joy and creates an atmosphere for victory. When we are filled with thanksgiving, we guard our hearts against doubt and give God room to work in our lives.

> Complaining creates an atmosphere for worry and anxiety.

When Moses led the Israelites through the wilderness, he experienced fear on several occasions. See how Moses expressed his fear to God and how God responded:

> Moses said to the Lord, "You have been
> telling me, 'Lead these people,' but you have
> not let me know whom you will send with
> me. You have said, 'I know you by name
> and you have found favor with me.' If you
> are pleased with me, teach me your ways so
> I may know you and continue to find favor
> with you. Remember that this nation is your
> people." The Lord replied, "My Presence
> will go with you, and I will give you rest."
>
> Exodus 33:12–14

It seems that Moses kept wanting to know who God would send to help him accomplish the assignment God had given him, but God wanted Moses to know that He would be with him and that was all he needed.

When we have God's presence, we have the answers to our problems and all the power we need to defeat our enemies. The psalmist David said God's presence was the "one thing" he would seek and ask for (Psalm 27:4). As we know from reading the Psalms, David had many enemies and fought many battles. I am sure he had learned that no matter what he had, if he didn't have God's presence, he didn't have what he needed to win.

We also see in the Psalms that David was a worshipper and frequently gave thanks to the Lord. For example, Psalm 95:2 (ESV) says, "Let us come into his presence with thanksgiving; let us make a joyful noise to him with songs of praise!" This is only one of many scriptures in which David writes of giving thanks. Instructions to give thanks and to be thankful are like a thread running not only through the Psalms but throughout the entire Bible. The giving of thanks is certainly an important subject for us to study and meditate on. If we want to enjoy God's presence, we need to create an atmosphere in which He will be comfortable—one of peace, gratitude, and faith.

When It's Easy and When It's Hard

We are to give thanks at all times and in all situations. When life is good and things are going our way, we find being thankful easy. But what about when life is hard? We see the apostle Paul and Silas expressing thankfulness in a very difficult time, and this should be our goal also:

> About midnight Paul and Silas were praying and singing hymns to God, and the other

prisoners were listening to them. Suddenly there was such a violent earthquake that the foundations of the prison were shaken. At once all the prison doors flew open, and everyone's chains came loose. The jailer woke up, and when he saw the prison doors open, he drew his sword and was about to kill himself because he thought the prisoners had escaped. But Paul shouted, "Don't harm yourself! We are all here!"

The jailer called for lights, rushed in and fell trembling before Paul and Silas. He then brought them out and asked, "Sirs, what must I do to be saved?"

They replied, "Believe in the Lord Jesus, and you will be saved—you and your household." Then they spoke the word of the Lord to him and to all the others in his house. At that hour of the night the jailer took them and washed their wounds; then immediately he and all his household were baptized. The jailer brought them into his house and set a meal before them; he was filled with joy because he had come to believe in God—he and his whole household.

Acts 16:25–34

> *Their prison doors were opened while they were praying and singing, not while they were complaining and doubting God.*

Their prison doors were opened while they were praying and singing, not while they were complaining and doubting God.

This account of praising God when praising Him is hard shows the power of gratitude. Because Paul and Silas remained thankful, not only were they set free, but the jailers and their households were saved and baptized. Those jailers witnessed a type of power they were unaccustomed to and knew that Paul and Silas had something they wanted and needed.

We have many problems in our world today. I think it is possible that all the complaining we do and all the negative, ungrateful talk we hear could be the root of many of those problems. We open a door to our enemy, the devil, through complaining. Just imagine how situations could change if everyone was thankful in all circumstances and we heard praise and thanksgiving to God, instead of grumbling and complaining, on a regular basis.

When Paul wrote the Book of Philippians, he

was imprisoned and held in chains, but he kept a good attitude. He says in Philippians 1:12–14:

> What has happened to me has actually served to advance the gospel. As a result, it has become clear throughout the whole palace guard and to everyone else that I am in chains for Christ. And because of my chains, most of the brothers and sisters have become confident in the Lord and dare all the more to proclaim the gospel without fear.

A few verses later, Paul writes, "I rejoice. Yes, and I will continue to rejoice, for I know that through your prayers and God's provision of the Spirit of Jesus Christ what has happened to me will turn out for my deliverance" (Philippians 1:18–19).

We can easily see through these examples that gratitude is a weapon, but weapons do us no good if we don't use them. I urge you to fill your days with the power of thank you when it is easy and when it is hard and to be thankful for little things as well as big things.

Thank-You Days

Bringing gratitude and thanksgiving into our daily lives will benefit us greatly, and it will help us defeat the enemy. One way to do it is to set aside an entire day occasionally and dedicate it to thanking God for each blessing you encounter throughout the day. Thank Him for modern conveniences that make your life easier and for food to eat, a place to live, friends and family, clean water to drink, and a comfortable bed. Many people in our world do not have even these basic blessings. Our ministry has been privileged, with the help of our partners, to provide nearly sixteen hundred water wells to villages in countries where people don't have clean water. In some of these places, they must walk miles even to get dirty water.

If you don't think you could dedicate an entire day to thanking God, then start small and dedicate the first fifteen minutes of every Monday, or whatever day you choose, simply to thank God for everything He provides that we tend to take for granted. However you decide to do it, find a way to develop the habit of being more thankful.

The Power of Thank You in Relationships

Healthy relationships seem to be getting more difficult to maintain than ever, and the enemy is busy at work trying to destroy them. More and more couples are divorcing, and in our world today we see less unity than ever before. Strife, offense, bitterness, resentment, and unforgiveness are rampant. I believe that saying thank you more often would eliminate at least a large part of the trouble we see in relationships. I actually believe that more gratitude instead of faultfinding in relationships would prevent thousands of divorces.

It is easy to find fault with others, but in the process of doing so, we often forget about our own faults. We expect other people to be merciful and not so easily offended, but we should give to others what we expect to get from them. Let me ask you a question: Right this moment, are you angry with anyone? Are you offended at anyone? Are you harboring deep-seated resentment toward someone, and has it been a part of your life for so long that you no longer even recognize it as a problem? If so, the best favor you can do for yourself is to forgive completely and find something to be thankful for about the person with whom you are angry. Ask God to help you forgive them, and find qualities that you do like about them. Thank God for anyone who has hurt you and pray for God to bless them. Before long, your feelings toward that person will change.

If you are in a relationship that is in trouble, start expressing gratitude for the other person's good traits and keep quiet about their faults. Always remember that we all have faults, but mercy is greater than judgment (James 2:13). Pray about what bothers you, and let God take care of your problems.

> Pray about what bothers you, and let God take care of your problems.

When God challenged me in this area, I thought about my dad and didn't see how I could find anything to be thankful for about him, but I did. There were a great many things he didn't do for me and a great many bad things he did to me, but he did give me a place to live, food to eat, and clothes to wear, and he sent me to school.

Learning to find something to be thankful for concerning him was part of my healing. Being thankful is so powerful that it will help to heal your wounded soul. The devil wants to throw you in a pit and keep you there

> Being thankful will help to heal your wounded soul.

the rest of your life through hating and resenting the people who hurt you, but Jesus came to open prison doors and lift people out of hopelessness and despair.

> He sends forth His word and heals them and
> rescues them from the pit and destruction.
> Psalm 107:20 AMPC

I strongly encourage you to let today be a new beginning for you—a place where you start fresh, letting go of what lies behind and beginning anew with an attitude of gratitude and thanksgiving.

CONCLUSION

I pray that I have written in this book exactly what you needed to read to help you see how important the power of thank you is. An attitude of gratitude is beautiful, and it is an attitude that people are drawn to. Nobody has fun being around a grouch who manages to find fault with almost everything and everyone, but people do enjoy being around someone who is positive and grateful.

The Bible says that we are to be lights in a dark world, and one easy way we can bring light is to have thankful hearts and express our gratitude as much as possible.

> Do all things without grumbling and fault-finding and complaining [against God] and questioning and doubting [among yourselves], that you may show yourselves to be blameless and guileless, innocent and uncontaminated, children of God without

blemish (faultless, unrebukable) in the midst of a crooked and wicked generation [spiritually perverted and perverse], among whom you are seen as bright lights (stars or beacons shining out clearly) in the [dark] world.

Philippians 2:14–15 AMPC

Not only is an attitude of gratitude pleasing to the Lord, but it has many benefits for us also. We will be happier and healthier, have more friends, and experience more promotion in life. Remember to "be thankful and say so" (Psalm 100:4 AMPC). We can never say thank you too often.

Simply thinking of and searching for things to be thankful for makes me happy. I believe that as you experience the power of thank you, you will be amazed at the difference it makes in your life. I encourage you to read this book again and again and to tell others about it. Underline sections that specifically speak to your heart and flip through the pages occasionally, reading only those parts. I encourage you to do this because repetition is the key to forming habits, and you will never regret the habit of gratitude.

I am excited for you because I believe that no matter how thankful you may have been before reading this book, you will be even more thankful now. I will pray for you, and I ask that you pray for me so that together we can be the most thankful people on earth.

APPENDIX:
THIRTY DAYS OF
THANK YOU

The scriptures below suggest specific things for which you can thank God. If you focus on one of these each day, you will have spent an entire month thanking God, and you can start again the next month. For months with thirty-one days, I challenge you to find one scripture that means something personal to you and use that as your thank you for those days.

Scripture uses several words to communicate the general idea of thanking God—including *praise*, *bless*, *rejoice*, *extol*, and *exalt*, depending on the Bible translation you read. When you see these words or similar ones in the verses below, remember that to praise God or to bless Him includes thanking Him.

1. Give thanks in all circumstances; for this is God's will for you in Christ Jesus (1 Thessalonians 5:18).

2. Give thanks to the Lord, for he is good; his love endures forever (1 Chronicles 16:34).

3. Let the peace of Christ rule in your hearts, since as members of one body you were called to peace. And be thankful (Colossians 3:15).

4. I praise you because I am fearfully and wonderfully made; your works are wonderful, I know that full well (Psalm 139:14).

5. Do not be anxious about anything, but in every situation, by prayer and petition, with thanksgiving, present your requests to God (Philippians 4:6).

6. And whatever you do, whether in word or deed, do it all in the name of the Lord Jesus, giving thanks to God the Father through him (Colossians 3:17).

7. Praise our God, all peoples, let the sound of his praise be heard; he has preserved our lives and kept our feet from slipping (Psalm 66:8–9).

8. Devote yourselves to prayer, being watchful and thankful (Colossians 4:2).

9. I will give thanks to the Lord because of his righteousness; I will sing the praises of the name of the Lord Most High (Psalm 7:17).

10. Then Hannah prayed and said: "My heart rejoices in the Lord; in the Lord my horn is lifted high. My mouth boasts over my enemies, for I delight in your deliverance. There is no one holy like the Lord; there is no one besides you; there is no Rock like our God" (1 Samuel 2:1–2).

11. Therefore, since we are receiving a kingdom that cannot be shaken, let us be thankful, and so worship God acceptably with reverence and awe, for our "God is a consuming fire" (Hebrews 12:28–29).

12. Praise the Lord, my soul, and forget not all his benefits—who forgives all your sins and heals all your diseases, who redeems your life from the pit and crowns you with love and compassion, who satisfies your desires with good things so that your youth is renewed like the eagle's (Psalm 103:2–5).

13. I always thank my God as I remember you in my prayers (Philemon 4).

14. I will praise you, Lord, with all my heart; before the "gods" I will sing your praise. I will bow down toward your holy temple and will praise your name for your unfailing love and your faithfulness, for you

have so exalted your solemn decree that it surpasses your fame. When I called, you answered me; you greatly emboldened me. May all the kings of the earth praise you, Lord, when they hear what you have decreed. May they sing of the ways of the Lord, for the glory of the Lord is great (Psalm 138:1–5).

15. I will give thanks to you, Lord, with all my heart; I will tell of all your wonderful deeds. I will be glad and rejoice in you; I will sing the praises of your name, O Most High (Psalm 9:1–2).

16. You are my God, and I will praise you; you are my God, and I will exalt you (Psalm 118:28).

17. But thanks be to God! He gives us the victory through our Lord Jesus Christ (1 Corinthians 15:57).

18. Let them give thanks to the Lord for his unfailing love and his wonderful deeds for mankind (Psalm 107:8).

19. I thank Christ Jesus our Lord, who has given me strength, that he considered me trustworthy, appointing me to his service (1 Timothy 1:12).

20. We praise you, God, we praise you, for your Name is near; people tell of your wonderful deeds (Psalm 75:1).

21. I urge, then, first of all, that petitions, prayers, intercession and thanksgiving be made for all people (1 Timothy 2:1).

22. Praise be to the Lord, for he has heard my cry for mercy (Psalm 28:6).

23. Let the message of Christ dwell among you richly as you teach and admonish one another with all wisdom through psalms, hymns, and songs from the Spirit, singing to God with gratitude in your hearts (Colossians 3:16).

24. I will praise you, Lord, among the nations; I will sing of you among the peoples. For great is your love, reaching to the heavens; your faithfulness reaches to the skies (Psalm 57:9–10).

25. So then, just as you received Christ Jesus as Lord, continue to live your lives in him, rooted and built up in him, strengthened in the faith as you were taught, and overflowing with thankfulness (Colossians 2:6–7).

26. The Lord is my strength and my defense; he has become my salvation. He is my

God, and I will praise him, my father's
God, and I will exalt him (Exodus 15:2).

27. Sing the praises of the Lord, you his faithful people; praise his holy name. For his
anger lasts only a moment, but his favor
lasts a lifetime; weeping may stay for the
night, but rejoicing comes in the morning
(Psalm 30:4–5).

28. But thanks be to God, who always leads
us as captives in Christ's triumphal pro-
cession and uses us to spread the aroma of
the knowledge of him everywhere (2 Corinthians 2:14).

29. Praise be to the God and Father of our
Lord Jesus Christ, the Father of compassion and the God of all comfort (2 Corinthians 1:3).

30. Praise be to the God and Father of our
Lord Jesus Christ, who has blessed us in
the heavenly realms with every spiritual
blessing in Christ. For he chose us in him
before the creation of the world to be holy
and blameless in his sight (Ephesians
1:3–4).

ENDNOTES

1. Krissy [no last name], "A Story of Gratitude and Heartfelt Thanks," *My Soulful Healing* (blog), November 22, 2012, https://mysoulfulhealing.wordpress.com /2012/11/22/a-story-of-gratitude-and -heartfelt-thanks/.
2. Marc Chernoff, "18 Great Reminders When You're Having a Bad Day," *Marc and Angel Hack Life* (blog), October 19, 2014, https://www.marcandangel.com/2014 /10/19/18-great-reminders-when-youre -having-a-bad-day.
3. Tim Dilena, *The 260 Journey* (Colorado Springs: Book Villages, 2021).
4. Ocean Robbins, "The Neuroscience of Why Gratitude Makes Us Healthier," *HuffPost*, January 4, 2012. https://www.huffpost.com /entry/having-gratitude-_b_1073105.
5. Nick Ortner, "A Short Lesson on Gratitude," The Tapping Solution (website),

n.d., https://www.thetappingsolution.com
/blog/short-lesson-gratitude.

6. "Keanu Helps Janitor Tidy Up His Life,"
Swept (website), March 2, 2020, https://
www.sweptworks.com/blog/industry-news
/keanu-helps-janitor.

7. "Gratitude Story about a Janitor," Thank
-Your-Stars.com, n.d., https://www.thank
-your-stars.com/story-about-a-janitor.html.

8. Marc Chernoff, "10 Places Unhappy People
Search for Happiness," *Marc and Angel Hack
Life* (blog), January 15, 2014, https://www
.marcandangel.com/2014/01/15/10-places
-unhappy-people-search-for-happiness.

9. Andrew Murray, *Humility* (Repr.: Orlando:
Bridge-Logos, 2000).

10. Brent Detwiler, "The Fifty Fruits of Pride,"
Bethany Community Church, https://www
.bethanycommunitychurch.org/resources
/docs/1409-the_fifty_fruits_of_pride.pdf.

Do you have a real relationship with Jesus?

God loves you! He created you to be a special, unique, one-of-a-kind individual, and He has a specific purpose and plan for your life. And through a personal relationship with your Creator—God—you can discover a way of life that will truly satisfy your soul.

No matter who you are, what you've done, or where you are in your life right now, God's love and grace are greater than your sin—your mistakes. Jesus willingly gave His life so you can receive forgiveness from God and have new life in Him. He's just waiting for you to invite Him to be your Savior and Lord.

If you are ready to commit your life to Jesus and follow Him, all you have to do is ask Him to forgive your sins and give you a fresh start in the life you are meant to live. Begin by praying this prayer...

Lord Jesus, thank You for giving Your life for me and forgiving me of my sins so I can have a personal relationship with You. I am sincerely sorry for the mistakes I've made, and I know I need You to help me live right.

Your Word says in Romans 10:9, "If you declare with your mouth, 'Jesus is Lord,' and believe in your heart that God raised him from the dead, you will be saved" (NIV). I believe You are the Son of God and confess You as my Savior and Lord. Take me just as I am, and work in my heart, making me the person You want me to be. I want to live for You, Jesus, and I am so grateful that You are giving me a fresh start in my new life with You today.

I love You, Jesus!

It's so amazing to know that God loves us so much! He wants to have a deep, intimate relationship with us that grows every day as we spend time with Him in prayer and Bible study. And we want to encourage you in your new life in Christ.

Please visit joycemeyer.org/salvation to request Joyce's book *A New Way of Living*, which is our gift to you. We also have other free resources online to help you make progress in pursuing everything God has for you.

Congratulations on your fresh start in your life in Christ! We hope to hear from you soon.

ABOUT THE AUTHOR

Joyce Meyer is one of the world's leading practical Bible teachers. A *New York Times* bestselling author, Joyce's books have helped millions of people find hope and restoration through Jesus Christ. Joyce's program, *Enjoying Everyday Life*, airs around the world on television, radio, and the internet. Through Joyce Meyer Ministries, Joyce teaches internationally on a number of topics with a particular focus on how the Word of God applies to our everyday lives. Her candid communication style allows her to share openly and practically about her experiences so others can apply what she has learned to their lives.

Joyce has authored more than 130 books, which have been translated into 155 languages, and over 65 million of her books have been distributed worldwide. Bestsellers include *Power Thoughts*; *The Confident Woman*; *Look Great, Feel Great*; *Starting Your Day Right*; *Ending Your Day Right*; *Approval Addiction*; *How to*

Hear from God; *Beauty for Ashes*; and *Battlefield of the Mind*.

Joyce's passion to help hurting people is foundational to the vision of Hand of Hope, the missions arm of Joyce Meyer Ministries. Hand of Hope provides worldwide humanitarian out-reaches such as feeding programs, medical care, disaster-relief efforts, human trafficking inter-vention and rehabilitation, and much more—always sharing the love and Gospel of Christ.

JOYCE MEYER MINISTRIES

U.S. & FOREIGN OFFICE ADDRESSES

Joyce Meyer Ministries
P.O. Box 655
Fenton, MO 63026
USA
(636) 349-0303

Joyce Meyer Ministries—Canada
P.O. Box 7700
Vancouver, BC V6B 4E2
Canada
(800) 868-1002

Joyce Meyer Ministries—Australia
Locked Bag 77
Mansfield Delivery Centre
Queensland 4122
Australia
(07) 3349 1200

Joyce Meyer Ministries—England
P.O. Box 1549
Windsor SL4 1GT
United Kingdom
01753 831102

Joyce Meyer Ministries—South Africa
P.O. Box 5
Cape Town 8000
South Africa
(27) 21-701-1056

Joyce Meyer Ministries—Francophonie
29 avenue Maurice Chevalier
77330 Ozoir la Ferriere
France

Joyce Meyer Ministries—Germany
Postfach 761001
22060 Hamburg
Germany
+49 (0)40 / 88 88 4 11 11

Joyce Meyer Ministries—Netherlands
Lorenzlaan 14
7002 HB Doetinchem
+31 657 555 9789

Joyce Meyer Ministries—Russia
P.O. Box 789
Moscow 101000
Russia
+7 (495) 727-14-68

OTHER BOOKS BY JOYCE MEYER

100 Inspirational Quotes
100 Ways to Simplify Your Life
21 Ways to Finding Peace and Happiness
Any Minute
Approval Addiction
The Approval Fix
Authentically, Uniquely You*
The Battle Belongs to the Lord
Battlefield of the Mind*
Battlefield of the Mind Bible
Battlefield of the Mind for Kids
Battlefield of the Mind for Teens
Battlefield of the Mind Devotional
Battlefield of the Mind New Testament
Be Anxious for Nothing*
Being the Person God Made You to Be
Beauty for Ashes
Change Your Words, Change Your Life
Colossians: A Biblical Study
The Confident Mom
The Confident Woman
The Confident Woman Devotional
Do It Afraid*
Do Yourself a Favor . . . Forgive
Eat the Cookie . . . Buy the Shoes

Seven Things That Steal Your Joy
Start Your New Life Today
Starting Your Day Right
Straight Talk
Strength for Each Day
Teenagers Are People Too!
Trusting God Day by Day
The Word, the Name, the Blood
Woman to Woman
You Can Begin Again
Your Battles Belong to the Lord*

JOYCE MEYER SPANISH TITLES

Auténtica y única (Authentically, Uniquely You)
Belleza en lugar de cenizas (Beauty for Ashes)
Buena salud, buena vida (Good Health, Good Life)
Cambia tus palabras, cambia tu vida (Change Your Words, Change Your Life)
El campo de batalla de la mente (Battlefield of the Mind)
Cómo envejecer sin avejentarse (How to Age without Getting Old)
Como formar buenos habitos y romper malos habitos (Making Good Habits, Breaking Bad Habits)
La conexión de la mente (The Mind Connection)
Dios no está enojado contigo (God Is Not Mad at You)
La dosis de aprobación (The Approval Fix)

Efesios: Comentario biblico (Ephesians: Biblical Commentary)

Empezando tu día bien (Starting Your Day Right)

Hágalo con miedo (Do It Afraid)

*Hazte un favor a ti mismo...perdona
(Do Yourself a Favor...Forgive)*

Madre segura de sí misma (The Confident Mom)

*Momentos de quietud con Dios
(Quiet Times with God Devotional)*

Pensamientos de poder (Power Thoughts)

*Sanidad para el alma de una mujer
(Healing the Soul of a Woman)*

Santiago: Comentario bíblico (James: Biblical Commentary)

Sobrecarga (Overload)

Sus batallas son del Señor (Your Battles Belong to the Lord)

Termina bien tu día (Ending Your Day Right)

Usted puede comenzar de nuevo (You Can Begin Again)

Viva valientemente (Living Courageously)

*Study Guide available for this title

BOOKS BY DAVE MEYER

Life Lines